MACARTHUR'S BLOODY BUTCHERS

Company G, 163rd Infantry Regiment, in the Pacific War

BRIAN BRUCE

CASEMATE

Pennsylvania & Yorkshire

Published in the United States of America and Great Britain in 2024 by
CASEMATE PUBLISHERS
1950 Lawrence Road, Havertown, PA 19083, USA
and
47 Church Street, Barnsley, S70 2AS, UK

Hardcover Edition: 978-1-63624-419-8
Digital Edition: 978-1-63624-420-4

A CIP record for this book is available from the British Library

Printed and bound in the United Kingdom by CPI Group (UK) Ltd, Croydon, CR0 4YY
Typeset in India by DiTech Publishing Services

For a complete list of Casemate titles, please contact:

CASEMATE PUBLISHERS (US)
Telephone (610) 853-9131
Fax (610) 853-9146
Email: casemate@casematepublishers.com
www.casematepublishers.com

CASEMATE PUBLISHERS (UK)
Telephone (0)1226 734350
Email: casemate@casemateuk.com
www.casemateuk.com

Cover image: A Sherman tank equipped with a bulldozer blade advances into the hills near
Zamboanga, accompanying men of the 163rd Infantry, March 1945. (National Archives)

MACARTHUR'S BLOODY BUTCHERS

For My Father

Company G's Pacific War. (Map created by Sonya Unrein)

Contents

Acknowledgements

My Uncle Doyle was a larger-than-life figure in my childhood even before I knew anything about his service in World War II. My father worked for him as a mason's assistant when he was a teenager and frequently told stories about Uncle Doyle's toughness, fairness, sense of humor, and commitment to doing the best job that could be done. He was a man of faith who loved his family and his community. All those aspects of his character are evident in his service to his country during his time as an infantryman fighting in the Pacific. He was a remarkable man.

Several people played important roles in helping me discover more about my Uncle Doyle's wartime experiences and in leading me to other sources and other men who served alongside him in Company G. Sally Slack Clifton conducted and recorded the interview with my uncle that was the catalyst for the other research that led to this book. My cousin, Doyle Edward Bruce Jr., made a transcript of that interview and published it, along with some of my Uncle Doyle's other writings about the war and other things, in a book titled *Doyle Edward Bruce 1916–1999: A Common Man of the Greatest Generation*. That book was invaluable. My aunt Helen Bruce, Uncle Doyle's wife, met with me on a wet December afternoon more than a decade ago and generously shared stories about how she met my uncle, and their lives together. She also gave me the books by Westerfield and Anderson that made this book possible. She was lovely, gregarious, and kind to me my entire life.

Hargis Westerfield, the official 41st Division Historian, wrote hundreds of articles about Company G and the entire 41st Division that were published in a newsletter that he wrote and edited for decades. Many of them were collected in *41st Infantry Division: Fighting Jungleers II*.

Westerfield's writing, based on his own personal experiences as well as the experiences of dozens of others and the records of the 41st Division and the 162nd, 163rd, and 186th Regiments, covered every aspect of the 41st's fight against the Japanese from the experiences of infantry units to quartermaster units and military policemen to artillerymen. His attention to detail and unique writing style brought the events of Company G's fight to life. It is impossible to imagine writing anything about any unit that was a part of the 41st Division without consulting his work.

Jack Anderson and my Uncle Doyle were good friends during the war and kept in touch in the decades that followed. Anderson's book, *Warrior ...By Choice ...By Chance* is a warm, honest, and sometimes funny account of his experiences during World War II. Anderson's deep knowledge of small-unit combat and his experience as squad and platoon leader on many patrols and during numerous engagements provided firsthand insights into the actions of Company G from the jungles of New Guinea to the ridges of Biak. His book also provides insight into the kind of young men he and my uncle were, which helped make this book more than just a recitation of battles and firefights.

I found Bruce L. Baird, the fourth member of Company G that this book follows, through the Library of Congress's Veterans History Project. He gave an interview that became a part of that collection, which is an amazing resource for anyone with an interest in World War II. In addition, he wrote his own version of the story of his time with Company G that includes valuable information about medical facilities, food, and the daily life of the men during their time in the South Pacific. His story enriched the story I attempt to tell in this book in ways that the records of the other men could not.

In addition to these primary sources there were three books that provided much of the information that I relied on for details and context. The official history of the 41st Division written by William F. McCartney, *The Jungleers: A History of the 41st Division*, provided me with the necessary overview of the actions of the 163rd Regiment and Company G as well as providing detailed information about troop movements, objectives, dates, and outcomes. "Hurricane at Biak: McArthur Against the Japanese May–August 1944" by Marc D. Bernstein contains a clear and detailed description of the U.S. battle for control of the island of Biak and the role played by the 163rd Infantry. Martin J. Kidston's book *From Poplar to Papua: Montana's 163rd Infantry Regiment in World War II* broadened my understanding of the experiences the men of the 163rd Regiment by including stories and anecdotes from soldiers other than the four men whose stories are at the heart of this book.

Several people who I know made valuable contributions to this book. My friend Dianne Hanegan kindly read and proofread the first completed version of the manuscript. Her patience with my poor understanding of comma rules and inability to understand when to use the word further instead of farther were much appreciated and all her contributions improved this book immensely. My sister Shelley Tatum was kind enough to read the original manuscript and offer her insights and suggestions, which was brave considering the condition of the text when I gave it to her and the danger of offering advice to a sibling. Her comments and enthusiasm for my project helped me to keep working at a critical juncture. My mother Sharon Bruce, who is almost always my first proofreader, also read the manuscript and offered me encouragement as she has throughout my life.

My friend Sonya Unrein created the excellent front-piece map showing Company G's path across the South Pacific. Her skill and talent made what was an idea I had for a map into a reality. Several friends I have met through BookTube have expressed interest, offered their encouragement, and occasionally an inspirational kick in the pants during the long process of writing this book. Special thanks to Allen, Marc, Hannah, Steve, Matt, Sonya, Marian, Jennie, Joe O/T Lautrec, Robert, Jeremy, Christy, Heidi, Doris, Greg, Britta, Gareth, Shawn, Karen, Jack, Margaret, Charlie B., Charlie H., Wiebke, Stephanie, Sandy, Melissa, Roz, Pat, Tess, Jenni J, Ami, Melissa Amy, Scott, Sarah, Lillian, Amy, Mark, Joni, Kelly, Jen, Kim, Pae, and Holly.

This book would not have been possible without the existence of the collections of two institutions and their staffs. Thank you to Zoe Ann Stoltz, the reference historian at the Montana Historical Society Research Center, and to Kelly Rovegno at Utah State University Special Collections and Archives.

A very special thanks to the staff at Casemate Publishers, particularly Ruth Sheppard, Lizzy Hammond, Declan Ingram, and Daniel Yesilonis for their professionalism and patient kindness in answering my many questions. Additional thanks to the editorial team of Elke Morice-Atkinson, Chris McNab, and Tracey Mills.

Thanks to my son, Ben, and daughter, Hannah, for teaching their father about strength, character, and general goodness—characteristics they share with their grandfather. Never-ending thanks and love to my wonderful wife Terri, who provided love, patience, kindness, support, understanding, and occasional technical assistance that made this and all things possible.

I wrote this book for my father, Victor Bruce Jr., who is responsible for my love of history and who tried his best to pass on the values he learned from Uncle Doyle to me. He read the original manuscript and I hope that the book in its final form would have pleased him.

Introduction

I was unaware that my Great Uncle Doyle had served in the United States Army and fought in the Pacific during World War II until an article about World War II veterans appeared in my hometown newspaper that featured my uncle's story. Even after that I never thought to ask him any questions about his experiences. We did not see each other regularly, and when we did, questioning him about the war did not seem appropriate. Then around 2006, after my uncle's death, my father loaned me a VHS tape that contained an interview that my uncle had given to another family member who was trying to preserve the memories of World War II veterans to whom she was related. I watched the tape and was moved by my uncle's openness, the clarity of his memory, and the horrors he had experienced during the war. I watched the tape a second time and recorded his answers and responses with a view toward writing something about his military service. That began a low-key and slow-evolving research and writing project which has resulted in this book.

I had only a vague idea of the actions of the U.S. Army during World War II in the Pacific. I knew army units fought in the Philippines and on Okinawa, but I had always thought of the war in the Pacific as a war fought mainly by the United States Marine Corps on islands like Guadalcanal, Peleliu, and Iwo Jima. The interview given by my uncle opened my eyes to a long, bitter, and no less significant part of the war. It was a war fought in the jungles of New Guinea, on the coral cliffs of Biak, the hills and ridges of Mindanao, and the mountainous islands of the Sulu Archipelago. Tens of thousands of American men fought in these places as members of infantry divisions like the 24th, the 32nd, and my uncle's division, the 41st.

Specifically, my Uncle Doyle served as a squad leader in the weapons platoon of Company G, 2nd Battalion, of the 163rd Infantry Regiment, of the 41st Infantry Division. That hierarchical, multi-unit designation highlights the complex and multilayered organization of the U.S. Army during World War II. Because this book references the movements and actions of the larger military structure that Company G was a part of, it is helpful to know a little bit about that structure.

At the beginning of the United States' involvement in World War II, an army division consisted of three infantry regiments, a headquarters company, four field artillery battalions, an artillery headquarters company, a tank destroyer battalion, a reconnaissance company, an engineer battalion, a quartermaster battalion, a signal company, a medical battalion, and an ordnance company. This organization made the division capable of independent action and largely self-supporting. The heart of any infantry division were the three infantry regiments. Like the division itself, each of those infantry regiments was made up of numerous constituent parts: three infantry battalions, a heavy weapons company, a headquarters company, and service companies. Within each infantry battalion there were four rifle companies, each of which was divided into three rifle platoons and a weapons platoon. Finally, each rifle platoon contained three rifle squads of nine to twelve men. Each squad contained a squad leader, a Browning Automatic Rifle or BAR man, and six to nine riflemen. The weapons platoon contained a light machine gun and a mortar section. The ranks of the officers in charge at each level were as follows: A regiment was led by a general, a battalion by a colonel, a company by a captain, a platoon by a lieutenant, and a squad by a sergeant.

The purpose of this complex organization and command structure was to allow semi-autonomous decision-making at each level to achieve the overall military objective of each group and the division as a whole. The officers and men, who had been trained in small group tactics, were expected to accomplish specific tasks without micromanagement from the upper levels. This meant that for any larger military strategy to succeed each individual soldier had to be able to do their job proficiently.

Every cliché that has been used to describe war applies to the war my uncle and the other men of Company G fought against the Japanese Imperial Army. During their time in combat, they became accustomed to pain, illness, stench, filth, muck, thirst, hunger, blood, gore, danger, cruelty, killing, and death. That people can learn to function in circumstances in which everything they have likely been taught to value and all the rules they have been taught to follow have been erased and in their place violence and killing have become virtues is part of the tragedy of war. Men in war do, and celebrate, things that in any other circumstance would be punished and a source of shame. That anyone emerges from time in combat and returns to the world mentally intact is remarkable. All wars are ugly. The war the United States fought to stop Japanese expansion in the Pacific and to destroy the Japanese Empire was no exception. When racism and punishing geography are added to the mix, war becomes even uglier.

This book focuses on the experiences of four members of Company G: Sergeant Jack Anderson, the son of a Montana rancher, who was with the company from its deployment through the Biak campaign; Sergeant Doyle Bruce from Texas, who was a member of the company from deployment through the Sulu Archipelago campaign; Sergeant Bruce Baird of Utah, who was with the company from the beginning but whose wounds and illnesses earned him enough points to rotate to the United States before the invasion of the Philippines; and Private Hargis Westerfield, who joined the company as a replacement after the Sanananda campaign and was with it until the end of the war.

Each of these men left behind an account of the war upon which this book depends. Over time, the exceptionally difficult circumstances under which they fought—the grinding cruelty, the daily danger, and extreme violence—numbed their sensibilities. As the war went on their accounts of what they saw and did became more matter of fact. What had seemed exceptional and memorable to them in the beginning became routine and unremarkable over time.

Just as each of these men learned to adapt to their circumstances and to become more expert and efficient soldiers, so did the U.S. military. When the men of Company G arrived in New Guinea in January 1943 the U.S. military was still working out issues of transport, supply, and strategy. As a result, the men did without much of the equipment, food, medicine, and the coordination of forces that would have made the fighting in New Guinea a little less nightmarish. By the time Company G landed on the Philippine island of Mindanao in 1945 the U.S. military could provide them with an abundance of new weapons and supplies as well as naval and air support that increased their advantage over their enemies.

Those advantages were welcome and undoubtedly saved American lives, but the war still came down to the determination and endurance of individual soldiers. The four soldiers whose experiences this book follows all dealt with the realities of the war and its aftermath differently, but they were all among the lucky. They survived the war and returned home to create lives, careers, and families. And each in his own way chose to preserve and record their experiences.

CHAPTER I

Before Deployment

December 7, 1941–April 6, 1942

When Jack Anderson was inducted into the U.S. Army on September 16, 1940, he was only sixteen years old. He had somehow managed to join the Montana National Guard the year before and thus was a member of the 163rd Infantry Regiment when it was folded into the 41st Division. He had already achieved the rank of corporal. Before 1940, Anderson and members of the 163rd looked and were equipped more like the Doughboys of World War I. They still wore the wide flat-brimmed hats of the Doughboys, carried 1903-model Springfield rifles, and had no motorized vehicles.[1] All that would change as the United States amped up its military preparedness in the wake of World War II in Europe and the Pacific and the 163rd joined the 41st Infantry Division.

The 41st Infantry Division of the U.S. Army participated in World War I and remained an official division in the years leading up to World War II. In the interwar years it transitioned to a division made up of National Guard units that drew its soldiers from the Northern Plains states and the Pacific Northwest. The division became active on September 16, 1940, the same day that President Franklin Roosevelt signed the Selective Training and Service Act into law. First assigned to Camp Murray, near Tacoma, Washington, the division began the logistical work of mustering out men ineligible for active service and welcoming draftees into its ranks. This was a confusing time within the division, whose total strength exceeded 21,000 men and included draftees still in need of training, as well as more experienced men in the process of going through advanced training. The division's strength would eventually return to normal and was further reduced as the army transitioned its infantry divisions from

Members of the 41st Division pose with a M1917A1 machine gun. Note the "sunset" division insignia shoulder patches. (Washington National Guard)

square divisions with four infantry regiments to triangular divisions with three regiments.[2]

The 163rd, made up of men from Montana, was notable for the large number of Native American men among its ranks. This unusual blending of the races created some unique situations for the men of the regiment who were unfamiliar with the customs and culture of their Sioux Indian comrades. The presence of so many Native Americans made the regiment such a source of curiosity for the citizens around Camp Murray that it even warranted a story in the *Tacoma Times*. The author of that story pointed out the irony of so many of the descendants of the men who had defeated Custer at the battle of the Little Bighorn now serving in the U.S. Army.[3]

For Anderson, the adjustment to life in a rough army camp that was still under construction proved somewhat easier than for his comrades who had not grown up on a Montana ranch. The men of the 41st had to construct their barracks themselves, fitting in construction time around their training schedule, and they slept on cots stuffed with straw which the army resupplied from time to time. The training at Camp

Murray concentrated on squad-level tactics. By the time the 163rd was first granted leave, Anderson was adept enough at those tactics that he was chosen to be one of the men who would help train the thousands of draftees who would be arriving at the equally new Fort Lewis which was located nearby. The move to the new facilities at Fort Lewis meant improved living conditions, but the work seemed endless. All the new equipment that poured into the base had to be catalogued, checked, and prepared for issuing to the new recruits. Anderson and the others also had to learn new combat techniques well enough to be able to instruct others. Promoted to sergeant, Anderson instructed the incoming soldiers on marksmanship, which was his specialty, as well as map reading and how to use a compass. When training ended Anderson rejoined Company G and found that many of the men he trained had replaced the longer-serving members of the company that had mustered out of the military.[4]

In his off-duty hours Anderson and the other men of Company G went into Tacoma in search of entertainment but did not always find the locals or the businesses there welcoming of soldiers. He did receive a warm welcome when he followed his mother's orders to visit the Hallock family that lived near the base. The Hallocks had at one time been neighbors of the Andersons in Montana and Anderson's mother and Mrs. Hallock had maintained a correspondence over the years. When Anderson traveled to the Hallocks' place he met Betty Hallock and the two began a friendship that burgeoned into love. On one of his last visits before deployment Anderson asked Betty to marry him. She accepted, but they agreed that they were still too young to marry and would wait until they were older. The war interrupted their plans, but they were eventually married.[5]

In the late summer and early fall of 1941, training at Fort Lewis took on a new intensity and took place on a new scale. The army scheduled several large maneuvers in the Pacific Northwest that included all the units of the 41st Division. These included the Hunter Liggett Reservation Maneuvers that went on from May to July of 1941 and then the Olympic Peninsula War Games that lasted from August till September of 1941. The division distinguished itself in both sets of maneuvers and emerged as one of the best-trained military units in the U.S. Army at that time.[6]

Doyle Bruce received word from the draft board that he would be drafted in early 1941. He was twenty-five and working in a Southern Pacific warehouse in Houston, Texas, at the time earning twenty dollars a week. He stayed on at his job through September of that year and was inducted into the U.S. Army on October 6, 1941. After a short trip home to say goodbye to his parents and siblings in Lufkin, Texas, where he left his 1940 Willys Coupe, his brother and his sister-in-law drove him back to Houston where he caught a train to San Antonio. After ten days going through the induction process the army shipped him to Camp Roberts, California, for basic training. The Japanese attack on Pearl Harbor resulted in Bruce and the other men being issued rifles and assigned to their military units. Bruce's orders took him north to Fort Lewis where he joined Company G.[7]

Bruce Baird was also drafted. He had been taking a break from Weber Junior College and was working in a U.S. Army depot when he got his draft notice. In August, the navy offered Baird the chance to join their officer training program, leaving him with a choice. As Baird saw things

Doyle Edward Bruce standing next to his 1940 Willys Coupe before being drafted into the military. (Collection of Sharon Bruce)

in 1941 the army was preferable because he believed that he would only have to serve for one year while as an officer in the navy he would have to serve at least three. So, in October he traveled to Fort Douglas in Salt Lake City where he was inducted into the army. He hoped that his two years studying science in college would earn him an advantageous assignment. It did not. From Fort Douglas Baird traveled to Camp Roberts, California, for basic training where he was issued a World War I-era rifle and gas mask. He was trained in how to use mortars, light machine guns, how to detect poison gas, and how to use a bayonet in combat. Baird and Doyle Bruce must have been at Camp Roberts at the same time, though not in the same training group.[8]

On December 7, 1941, the men of the 41st learned that the United States had been attacked. As news filtered in about the devastation at Pearl Harbor, the men of the 41st, as well as the rest of the country, also learned of Japanese attacks in the Philippines, Guam, Wake Island, and the Aleutian island chain. Fear spread that the Japanese were planning an attack on the West Coast of the United States. To guard against such an attack the men of the 41st spent several weeks on guard duty up and down the cold and wet coast of the Pacific Northwest.[9] After Pearl Harbor, Company G moved up the coast of Washington to Puget Sound Peninsula. There they moved into an old Civilian Conservation Corp camp made of slapped-together, tar-paper-covered barracks with only barrel heaters for warmth. Company G spent six cold, wet weeks patrolling the area before being sent back to Fort Lewis for more training.[10]

Bruce Baird had a pass to Los Angeles for the weekend of December 7, 1941. He and the other men in his group began the return journey to Camp Roberts that same day. At the train station Baird saw a Japanese family being escorted onto a train by armed security. The fear of a Japanese attack on the Pacific Coast forced the army to cut his group's training at Camp Roberts short. A few days after December 7 he boarded a train for Fort Lewis where he would become a member of Company G of the 163rd Regiment. As a member of Company G, Baird was assigned to guard Puget Sound at Port Angeles where they stayed when not on guard duty. When on duty, Baird and his squad lived in a low-roofed log structure with a non-waterproof tarp for a roof. Their sentry post consisted of a roll of barbed wire stretched across a crossroad leading to the coast and a foxhole in which a BAR man stood. The army delivered their meals by truck every day, but locals provided them with enough food and treats that Baird felt like they could have gotten along without the army food. Company commanders managed to scavenge equipment for the men who otherwise would have been without sleeping bags and other things that kept them warmer and drier. The sentry posts' communications equipment had been hooked into an area party line which meant the men could listen in on the locals' conversations and locals could listen in to the military communications coming into the sentry point.[11]

Doyle Edward Bruce at either Camp Roberts, California, or Camp Murray, Washington, wearing a World War I flat-brimmed hat. The flat-brimmed hat would be replaced by the time of his deployment to Australia. (Collection of Sharon Bruce)

In February of 1942, the 163rd received orders to travel by train to San Francisco in preparation for deployment overseas. They were given a series of shots to try to protect them from tropical diseases. Those shots would prove to be ineffective.[12] In San Francisco the men of the 163rd learned that they were to travel on the HMS *Queen Elizabeth* bound for an unknown destination. The *Queen Elizabeth* had been converted to a troop transport ship after the war started and was uniquely qualified for the job.[13] As the largest passenger ship in the world it could, when stripped of its luxurious amenities, carry thousands of men and travel at a speed of twenty-nine knots. This gave it the speed to outrun pursuing Japanese submarines and reduced the need for escort ships. On March 19 the men of the 163rd along with those of the 167th Field Artillery Battalion, Division Headquarters, the 41st Signal Company, 116th Engineer, Medical, and Quartermaster

Battalions boarded the *Queen Elizabeth*. Speculation about where they were going ran high because the 162nd Regiment had earlier entrained for the East Coast and the 186th Regiment had yet to receive orders to leave the United States.[14]

As the *Queen Elizabeth* left San Francisco, Doyle Bruce stood on deck along with all the men who could fit. As they sailed underneath the Golden Gate Bridge it seemed to Bruce like the bottom of the bridge was almost close enough to touch and he must have wondered when he would return home.[15] He and the others on board the *Queen Elizabeth* would not even learn they were bound for Australia until they reached the Marquesas, where they stopped to refuel halfway through their journey.

The men of Company G, like most of the other men of the 163rd, found life aboard the *Queen Elizabeth* to be less than luxurious. All the fine state rooms and ornate public spaces had been converted to bunk space for the men. Constructed from steel pipes and canvas straps, the bunks

The *Queen Elizabeth*, left—pictured alongside her sister ship, the *Queen Mary*—carried the men of the 163rd from San Francisco to Australia in the spring of 1942. (Anonymous)

were little more than rectangular sleeping platforms. These platforms were stacked three or four high with just enough room between the bunks for a man to crawl in and lay down. They were arranged in rows that were so close together that men passing one another in the aisles between them had to turn sideways to get by.[16] Baird spent the trip to Australia in a stateroom with three stacks of these metal and canvas bunks, four bunks high.[17]

All the fresh water on the ship was reserved for drinking and cooking, so each man got one canteen of water a day. This meant that bathing took the form of cold seawater showers which, along with the inadequate soap available, meant that the men rarely bothered. Most of the bunk areas on board the ship were well below decks and there was no way of ventilating them other than keeping doors and hatches open. As the ship traveled through the tropics and across the South Pacific, the air below deck became increasingly hot and fetid. The combination of poor hygiene, close quarters, and hot air created a remarkably bad smell that drove most of the men out onto deck most of the time.

The food also disappointed. There were no fresh fruits or vegetables, the only meat served was mutton of questionable age, and the flour was full of weevils. The cooks on board the ship were British and either boiled or steamed everything. Frequently, breakfast consisted of steamed tomatoes on toast and lunch of boiled meat and potatoes. Because of the number of men aboard the ship, the crew could only prepare and serve two meals a day and the men had to stand in line for an hour or longer to get them.[18] To speed up the meal service the men developed a system where one soldier from each table of twelve would go and get food for an entire table and bring it back.[19]

Doyle Bruce took advantage of the relative monotony of life onboard ship to do some exploring. On the upper decks he marveled at the ship's two swimming pools and tennis courts, though none of them were in use during the voyage. He admired the remaining wood paneling and chandeliers. Even with most of its finery stripped away, he considered the *Queen Elizabeth* to be the finest ship that ever sailed.[20]

Anderson's experience of life on board the *Queen Elizabeth* varied only slightly from that of most of the men of the 163rd. He had the good luck to be assigned to a former stateroom instead of getting a berth in one of the large common areas with their tiers of bunks. This proved to be a limited advantage because he shared the stateroom that was designed for double occupancy with eleven other men. The room had a porthole which did not open, so the only air that circulated in the room came from a vent in the hallway that only blew hot air. To escape the heat and the foul odors in his cabin he spent as much time as possible on deck where competition for space to lie down was fierce. He only spent time in his bunk in the cabin when it was time for sleep. Despite the comparative privacy of Anderson's accommodations onboard ship, the time he spent crossing the Pacific felt torturously slow and he blamed part of what he considered to be the roughness of their crossing on the fact that the ship was overloaded with men and supplies.[21]

For all three of the men from Company G the most impressive thing about the *Queen Elizabeth* as a troopship was the ship's speed. At the beginning of the journey the ship sailed at less than top speed, heading south parallel to the coast of South America before turning west, accompanied by a few other ships including the *President Coolidge* and the *Mariposa*. But as the *Queen Elizabeth* neared the International Date Line it left its companion ships behind and went at full speed for Australia, arriving at Sydney on April 6, 1942, having made the trip in just eighteen days. The journey was remarkably short thanks to there being no submarine scares, and the *Queen Elizabeth*'s speed. When the ship sailed into Sydney Harbor, the 163rd became the first element of the 41st to arrive in Australia.[22]

The 163rd's journey to its first base in Australia still had one stage left. They had docked at Sydney instead of their actual destination, Melbourne, because the *Queen Elizabeth* was too big for the dock facilities there. This meant all the men of the regiment and all their equipment had to be unloaded from the *Queen Elizabeth* and loaded onto smaller Dutch ships for the final leg of the journey. To complicate matters, the Javanese crews of the Dutch ships went on strike so the 2nd Battalion, which included the men of Company G, had to take over the role of longshoreman unloading equipment from the *Queen Elizabeth* and loading it on board the Dutch ships.[23] Eventually the Dutch captains convinced the Javanese crew members to board the ships and the 163rd minus the 2nd Battalion began the final leg of the journey to Melbourne. The journey across the Tasman Sea was very rough with high seas rocking the ships and huge waves crashing across the decks of the Dutch ships, which were much smaller than the *Queen Elizabeth*. An improvement in the food on board made the trip south more tolerable for the men of the 163rd. The Dutch ships kept live sheep and goats on board, which provided the men with fresh meat and milk. The Javanese crew members proved a curiosity for the American soldiers who found their music strange and their practice of eating the rice dishes (that made up most of their diet) with their fingers, odd. The trip only took three days and the 163rd arrived to find the docks in Melbourne thronged with Australians who were thrilled to have them in the country.[24] The 2nd Battalion made the long journey from Sydney to Melbourne by rail which gave Bruce a chance to see the Australian countryside. He did not see any kangaroos, but he did see some emus when the train stopped at stations along the route. The tedium of the journey was relieved by a steady supply of food, which was mostly mutton sausages on bread, and beer. Because he did not smoke, Bruce traded his cigarette allotment for beer, which likely made his journey more bearable.[25]

CHAPTER 2

Australia

April 6, 1942–December 25, 1942

Though Bruce, Anderson, and Baird missed the cheering crowds that greeted the other members of the 163rd and the other elements of the 41st Division on the docks at Melbourne, they understood how much relief their presence gave the people of Australia. With the rapid advance of Japanese forces in all directions the Australians had reason to fear a Japanese invasion.

Securing Australia became a priority for Allied military command early in 1942. As an ally Australia's military was making important contributions to the war in North Africa as well as the Pacific where they did yeoman's work slowing down Japanese advances in the South Pacific. In addition, Australia itself would prove a critical base for training, stationing, and resting U.S. soldiers during the war and as a jumping off point for the planned offensive against Japan. The Japanese had plans, perhaps overly ambitious plans, for spreading the empire to the south and taking over coastal Australia or, at the very least, preventing the United States from using Australia as a base for itself. In 1942 the Japanese Imperial Command put its plan to establish air bases in New Guinea and the Solomon Islands into action. These bases could be used to facilitate an invasion of Australia and, potentially, could cut off the sea lanes that connected Australia to the United States. With most of its military away fighting the war in North Africa, there were few Australian soldiers standing in their way and the people of Australia and its government prepared for invasion.[1]

Allied command had chosen the 41st Division to bolster the Australian defenses. Though the different elements of the division arrived piece-meal—the 163rd Regiment on April 6, followed by the 162nd Regiment on April 9, and finally the 186th Regiment on May 13—the entire 15,000-man strong division was in Australia by May of 1942.[2]

After making their way to Melbourne all elements of the 41st boarded trains for an old Australian army base located near the town of Seymour. This camp would be the division's home for several months while the men began training.[3] The camp itself consisted mainly of tents and the men had to sleep on the ground.[4] The terrain around their camp proved less than ideal to the men of the 41st. Hills covered with rock and sparse clumps of grass dominated the landscape. In the gravel-strewn flat lands thousands of sheep were set to graze by local shepherds. It rained and it was cold most of the days the division spent in their makeshift camp, which made staying dry and warm a challenge for the Americans.[5] Not surprisingly, the other thing the men of the 163rd complained about after reaching their camp at Seymour was the food. Their initial meals were prepared by Australian Army cooks who cooked mutton stew and brewed coffee in old oil drums. Sometimes the men got sheep carcasses, of questionable freshness, from which they made their own meals. After a few weeks the regiment's own cooks showed up and took over. Knowing the men did not care for mutton, the GI cooks traded it for beef and fresh bread. To the horror of the Americans who unloaded it, the bread often arrived at camp unwrapped and stacked in the bed of the same trucks that hauled garbage away from the camp.[6]

The Americans' training regimen consisted of long marches of up to thirty miles on consecutive days and technical weapons and combat training. According to Anderson these training hikes were so long and to such remote areas that Company G's field kitchens sometimes could not find them, which forced the men to eat hard tack (thick crackers) and canned meat of questionable age and origin.[7]

It was while they were stationed at Seymour that the men of the 41st were issued M1 rifles and new helmets to replace the World War I era equipment they brought with them from the United States.[8] As a member of Company G's weapons platoon Doyle Bruce learned how to use a 60mm mortar while stationed at the camp in Seymour. The mortar launched grenade-like shells in an arching trajectory towards enemy lines. It provided light artillery support for the men of the company and was effective in softening fixed enemy positions. Each mortar was operated by a three-man crew consisting of a non-commissioned officer who led each group and fired the weapon, and two privates. During marches or combat engagements in which mortars were not or could not be used, the mortar crew still had to carry the mortar and ammunition with them. One man carried the ammunition, one the tube that fired the shells, and the other a heavy metal plate to which the mortar was attached to provide stability. The items the mortar men carried were in addition to their sixty-pound packs and the relatively heavy M1 rifle they had each been issued. When mortars were not in use, the mortar men fought as the company's fourth rifle platoon.[9]

Bruce Baird received a promotion to corporal that brought with it more responsibility and pay. While stationed in Seymour Baird applied and was accepted for flight training in the Air Corps. He and the other men who qualified were told to be constantly packed and prepared for transfer back to the United States and flight school. But a few weeks after being accepted, division command informed Baird and the others that because of manpower issues no members of the 41st would be leaving Australia and returning to the United States.[10]

To break the monotony of camp life and the drudgery of hard training, the men of the 163rd looked for any source of entertainment. Newspapers from Melbourne and Sydney provided brief distraction, but also brought reminders that the war was going on and not going particularly well for the Allies.[11] At night the men played cards and some who had managed to bring musical instruments with them attempted to play music, a form of entertainment not always popular with all the men of the 163rd. One of the most common distractions was alcohol and many of the men of the 163rd spent a good deal of time searching for alcohol and drinking what they could find. The men found that Australian whiskey and beer were more potent than they were used to. This, and frequency of consumption, led of course to rowdy, if usually good-natured behavior, and the imposition of tighter military discipline.[12]

Passes to Melbourne provided the greatest chance for fun. The GIs stationed at Seymour enjoyed all that Melbourne had to offer, including rugby matches, a zoo, horse races, and boat trips up the St. Kilda River.[13] Because of the dietary restrictions Bruce Baird followed as a member of the Church of Jesus Christ of Latter-day Saints, food was often a problem for him. But Melbourne offered the chance to buy fruit, visit bakeries, and eat good meals in cafes.[14] In the city the American GIs learned to smoke Crave A cigarettes and developed a tolerance for the strong Australian beer. But the young women of Melbourne were the main attraction, and the women of Australia took to the American GIs right away. Apparently, the Americans were more attentive and solicitous dates than the women of Australia were used to. The GIs brought them gifts, took them out, and treated them better than the Australian men.[15] Anderson felt that because the GIs "wined and dined" the Australian women that many of them fell for American soldiers more seriously than they should have, considering all that most of the men were looking for was a good time. He also believed that the reason Australian men were resentful of the Americans' romantic successes was because they believed the Americans were spoiling the women.[16] The popularity of the Americans undoubtedly caused some tension with the local men. This took the form of challenging the Yanks to drinking contests in which the American GIs acquitted themselves well. Despite the tensions, there were only a few violent incidents—probably because most of the young Australian men from Melbourne were serving in their military elsewhere.[17]

The men of Company G endured the same hardships at the camp in Seymour as the other members of the 41st Division. They complained about the food, the cold, and the wet. They endured the same physically exhausting training and boredom. But Company G got lucky. Australian dockworkers were slow to unload the 41st Division's equipment and supplies as they arrived, which created a great deal of frustration with division command. That frustration grew exponentially worse when U.S. military police working the docks discovered that the dockworkers frequently helped themselves to U.S. military supplies. The workers brought huge lunch boxes to work with them each day and used them to conceal the things they stole. When U.S. military police confronted the leaders of the dockworkers' union about the issue, they refused to take any action. When the military police ordered the dockworkers to leave their lunch boxes outside the gates that led to the docks, the workers threatened to go on strike. The solution was for U.S. soldiers to work the docks unloading U.S. military supplies and equipment, a move which the Australian dockworkers could not effectively prevent. Company G was the unit selected to work the docks in Melbourne.[18]

The opportunity to live and work in Melbourne instead of at the military camp in Seymour made Company G the envy of the rest of the division. Though the work during their eight-hour shifts left them tired, the men of Company G enjoyed sixteen hours of freedom a day during which they could sleep, sightsee, go to the movies, eat in restaurants, drink in pubs, and mingle with the young women of Melbourne.[19] For Bruce Baird the highlight of working the Melbourne docks was being there when one of the other infantry regiments, probably the 186th which departed Fort Lewis last of all the infantry regiments that made up the 41st Division, arrived. The 162nd had departed Fort Lewis first heading east by train before being ordered to Australia with the rest of the division. The French luxury liner *Normandie* had been chosen to act as their transport ship, but when a fire on board destroyed it, the men of the 162nd boarded several smaller ships that sailed down the East Coast of the United States, passed through the Panama Canal, and crossed the Pacific. In all the regiment spent forty days at sea.[20]

Anderson's initial impressions of Australia centered on the challenges posed by trying to learn Australian English, being patient with the inefficient Australian rail service that made travel across the country slow and difficult, and adapting to the food. His attitude toward his time in Australia probably helped him to settle in and enjoy the experience faster than most, though his idea of having a good time was very different from that of most of the Americans of the 41st Division.

During Company G's stint as dockworkers in Melbourne, Anderson spent his free time exploring the city's theaters, parks, beaches, and the zoo. After his first few days as a substitute dock worker, Anderson figured out that if he traded shifts with other men he could explore outside the city as well. He took advantage of Melbourne's efficient electric streetcar system to visit surrounding communities. His favorite was Dandenong where he found a small community of friendly people. There an older woman, whose husband was serving in Africa, befriended Anderson, and he began to spend time at her horse ranch where she also raised wallabies and emus. In her husband's absence, the ranch had become run down and Anderson, in return for the chance to ride the horses and for introductions to local young women, worked the ranch when he could. Anderson's enjoyment of life in and around Melbourne ended when Company G was called back to the camp at Seymour.[21]

In July of 1942, the 41st Division received orders to move from Seymour to Rockhampton, near Australia's northeast coast.[22] The move resulted from General Douglas MacArthur's decision as overall Allied Commander in the Pacific to override the Australian military's decision to create an inland line of defense against a Japanese invasion. MacArthur believed that the best place to meet a Japanese invasion would be along the coast and threatened to resign his position unless he got his way. MacArthur got his way and the 41st was on the move again.[23]

But because of the inefficiency of the Australian railway system, the division crawled across the continent. Every time a train carrying elements of the 41st or its equipment crossed a territorial line all the men and equipment had to be moved from one train to another because of the different gauges of track used in each of the Australian territories. Doyle Bruce recalled this happening three times over the course of a trip that was over 400 miles long. The stops to change trains and the unloading and reloading of all the equipment made a tediously long journey even worse.[24] Bruce Baird had complaints about the food on the trip and the slow progress of the trains, but he had a method for escaping the crowded passenger cars when it was time to sleep.[25] At night he would walk through the train till he came to a flatbed car carrying tarp-covered equipment, slip under the tarp, and find a private place to sleep. Jack Anderson recalled that at one point, railway officials lost track of a train carrying men and supplies in the wilderness for more than a week.[26] Eventually all elements of the 41st arrived in Rockhampton.

Though still under construction, the U.S. military camp near Rockhampton had far more to offer the men than the camp at Seymour. Men at the former camp still slept in tents, but there were facilities for showering and kitchens in permanent structures. This meant the men were cleaner and there was a wider variety in the meals they ate. Though stews were still common they had one steak dinner a week, fruit juice was available, and there was ice cream, and baked goods.[27]

The men of the 163rd's first glimpse of Rockhampton inspired little hope for the continuation of the good times they had had in Melbourne. Rockhampton was a small town of around 1,500 people and, to make matters worse, the bars and restaurants had to water down the beer and whisky because it was in short supply. There were also fewer young women. The lack of entertainment and the necessity of drinking watered-down booze didn't prevent numerous instances of drunkenness or the occasional unwanted pregnancy, though.[28]

The good times the men of Company G had while off-duty occasionally affected their military duties. Corporal Baird found himself in charge of his squad from time to time while the sergeant was away for health reasons or had a pass. This led to several encounters with soldiers who spent their time, and not always their off-duty time, drunk. One night two soldiers, one of whom was on guard duty, snuck out of camp and took a jeep to retrieve a third squad member who had gotten drunk in a small town nearby. In a rush to get back before being discovered by Baird they drove too fast on a gravel road and ran into a tree. Two of the three men ended up in the hospital and the jeep was wrecked which forced Baird to file a report. A trial for the man who had been on guard duty was scheduled. A few weeks later that same soldier was drunk again and determined to report for guard duty. When Baird tried to stop him, the man approached him as though he were going to hit Baird with his rifle. Baird overpowered him and marched him back to his barracks to sleep it off. The soldier's trial took place several months later and because his guard duty was not classified as a regular military duty, he was fined fifty dollars instead of being court martialed.[29]

The 41st Division's base in Rockhampton brought them closer to where the Japanese southward advances were taking place, making the war more of a reality for the men of the 163rd. They knew that now the Japanese were only a few hundred miles away, threatening the island of New Guinea to their north and the Solomon Islands to their east. Their training became harder and more serious. They were taught jungle fighting skills and participated in maneuvers and training runs during which live shells and ammunition were used. New equipment of varying usefulness designed to aid them in the jungle was issued along with the

A soldier of the 41st Division demonstrates the technique for attacking an enemy machine-gun nest near Rockhampton, Australia, November 1942. (National Archives)

new cotton uniforms. They began receiving Atabrine pills, which were designed to prevent them from contracting malaria. Many of the men tossed these pills away because they turned their skin yellow—and many would later regret it.[30]

The men of Company G, like all the men in the division, spent their first few weeks in northern Australia moving equipment and supplies and setting up camp. The climate in Rockhampton was dramatically different from the division's first Australian base. Seymour was cold and rainy. Rockhampton was hot and dry. The difference in climate helped the men become somewhat accustomed to the conditions under which they would be fighting in the Pacific. It also brought about a change in uniforms worn on base. Gone were the olive drab wool uniforms and in their place, cotton khaki uniforms.[31] New gear was one of the highlights of the first few weeks in their new location.

However, not all the new uniform options were popular with the men. The army also issued each man a camouflaged one-piece uniform which zipped up the front. The men nicknamed this the "Army Zoot Suit" and quickly became acquainted with the "Zoot Suit"'s design flaws. It was hot and trapped sweat; its pockets were in places that interfered with the location of the standard army belt and its compartments. But worst of all, it did not have a trap door in the seat which meant that for a soldier to go to the bathroom they had to take the "Zoot Suit" off completely. Fortunately, the men were never required to wear it in combat. In addition to the new uniforms, the men also received some new gear that included a rain poncho that absorbed water instead of repelling it, a sleeping hammock that despite its effectiveness in shielding the men from rain and mosquitoes was too bulky and heavy to carry into combat, as well as hunting knives and machetes, which proved very useful.[32]

Shortly after arriving at Rockhampton, Company G left the main camp to conduct motorized patrols along the nearby coast. Each squad got additional communications equipment and a jeep to carry out high-speed patrols. They took advantage of their location to bathe and swim in the ocean, sample the high life during patrols through resort communities, and to visit villages of indigenous peoples. Baird gave some of the kids from these villages rides in his jeep and he and other men were treated to fresh produce and free time to hike or play volleyball on the beach. When not relaxing they mapped the area and made reports about the potential military usefulness of roads and trails.[33] That assignment did not last long, and Company G returned to the main camp where preparations for their deployment were under way.

At Rockhampton training became more specific. The men practiced amphibious landings and trained in jungle fighting techniques. Each regiment in the division practiced landing on the beaches near Toorbul Point (which the men nicknamed "Terrible Point") and then spent several weeks training along the Fitzroy River before being given a week of rest and relaxation on the beaches of Yeppoon. During this period of rest, Company G's commander Captain William "Wild Bill" Benson lived up to his nickname. He went out drinking with a group of Australian officers and, at some point, there was an altercation that resulted in Benson being thrown out of a second story window. He broke his leg but was back with the company before its first combat deployment.[34]

While at Rockhampton the division's artillery battalions were reorganized and trained to use new weapons and the engineering and quartermaster battalions were being drilled on new procedures developed at I Corps. In all the 41st Division spent more than six months training and equipping at Rockhampton in preparation for their first combat deployment.[35]

The 2nd Battalion excelled at battalion-level maneuvers in and around Rockhampton. The officers and men of the battalion earned the highest ratings for their practice amphibious landings at Toorbul Point and set a high bar for the other battalions of the division. As a part of the 2nd Battalion, Company G was among the first units to practice the techniques for amphibious assault on the beachhead at Toorbul Point. They practiced landing on the beach over and over again as live artillery shells

Members of the 41st Division practice climbing a cargo net to board landing craft near Rockhampton, Australia, November 1942. (National Archives)

streaked overhead.[36] They trained in rubber boats that they had to paddle to shore and then carry onto land with them. Whatever motorized landing craft the U.S. Army had at that time was allocated for use in the European theatre.[37] At the company level the men received small-group combat training and the ranks filled to capacity by an influx of new recruits and draftees that had begun to arrive in Australia.[38]

This next phase of training involved small units, sometimes a squad or smaller, on long-range patrols. On these patrols a group of men was transported in vehicles with blacked-out windows several miles out into the Australian bush country and dropped off. They were given a map, marked with checkpoints and the distance between them, and a compass and expected to navigate their way through each checkpoint until they reached their final destination. These challenging exercises, which required that each man learn how to navigate in unfamiliar ter-

Men of the 163rd practice amphibious landings at Toorbul Point, Australia, 1942–43. (National Archives)

ritory, paid real benefits when the 41st was sent into combat. They also emphasized the importance U.S. military command placed on the ability of small units to act independently to achieve larger group goals. For the men of Company G, the best part of these exercises was the food. The soldiers participating in the training were dropped off in the wilderness without food, but they knew that waiting for them at the last checkpoint would be mobile kitchens that served them steak and French fries and even a bottle of beer.[39]

After this training was complete, Company G was again chosen for a special assignment that took them away from base. This time they were sent to the small harbor town of Gladstone, located on the coast around 62 miles south of Rockhampton and close to the mouth of the Calliope River. Japanese submarines had been spotted in the waters nearby, raising fears of a Japanese attack or invasion. The move to Gladstone made Company G the first line of defense against any invasion of Australia. Though likelihood of a Japanese attack was slight, the presence of the American GIs made the citizens of Gladstone feel better.

Another company assigned to Gladstone earlier had completed the work of setting up defensive positions around the harbor, building artillery and anti-aircraft gun emplacements, so Company G's duties consisted of manning the guns, patrolling the beach and doing harbor watches. The men counted themselves lucky to have drawn such an easy assignment in such a welcoming place. At any given time only about a third of the men were on duty leaving more than one hundred men

Soldiers of 41st Division practice maneuvers in the Australian countryside near Rockhampton, Australia, 1942. (National Archives)

free and searching for fun, which the people of Gladstone were happy to oblige.

The town's lone movie theatre showed only Hollywood movies and changed movies once a week. But during Company G's time there, they held each movie over for an extra day so the men who had to be on duty at the time the theatre was open had a chance to see it the next week. The towns, pubs and restaurants did a booming business though the shortage of alcohol disappointed many of the company's drinkers. The stores stocked things that the Americans did not have access to on their base and the low prices allowed the men to augment what they were issued by buying items on their own. Twice a week the town hosted dances at the community hall where the Americans had a chance to mingle with the single, young women of Gladstone and the surrounding area. Because the GIs outnumbered the available women, there was a real competition at these dances and elsewhere. The men lucky enough to get dates found that their options for entertainment after the dance were severely limited and they usually ended up going to the home of one of the young women in their group for snacks and drinks.[40]

Doyle Bruce and Jack Anderson were among the men lucky enough to find regular dates in Gladstone. During the month Company G was assigned to Gladstone, Bruce became involved with a young local woman named June Connellan. June was in her early twenties with bright eyes, a broad smile, and somewhat frizzy red hair. Short by any standard, June Connellan and Bruce, who was six-foot-two, must have looked like a mismatched pair. A picture of June that Bruce kept shows her standing barefoot next to a fence wearing a short romper and sweater, holding a decent-sized trout in one hand and a fishing pole in the other. June's parents, Denis and Elizabeth "Dotty" Connellan, loved Bruce, and he was a frequent guest in their home. In return he helped them out with small jobs around the place.[41]

Jack Anderson, who loved to dance, looked forward to the dances organized for the soldiers by the people of Gladstone that he had heard others describe. Unfortunately, he developed a severe sinus infection just after the move to Gladstone and he missed the first few dances. By the time he was well enough to attend, most of the local young women had already paired off with an American soldier, leaving Anderson without a partner for a time. But at one of the dances, he noticed an attractive blonde woman sitting at a table with a short redhead and his good friend Doyle Bruce. He asked Bruce about her, and Bruce introduced him to Dorothy Henderson.

The forwardness of most of the American soldiers she had met put Henderson off. She had a fiancé serving in Africa and was not interested in what most of the American GIs were after. But she agreed to dance with Anderson and afterwards they talked. Dorothy, who was a few years older and had a job and her own apartment, impressed Anderson and he was determined to impress her. He told her about his fiancée

Doyle Edward Bruce in khaki uniform issued to the men of Company G in Rockhampton, Australia, in 1942. (Collection of Sharon Bruce)

and how they had promised to stay faithful to each other but agreed that they should each go out with other people while they were separated. This, and Anderson's regular church attendance, did impress Dorothy and she and Anderson became close companions throughout the time he was stationed in Gladstone.

As a result of their relationships with June and Dorothy, Bruce and Anderson became like the adopted sons of June's parents, who ran a boarding house in Gladstone. Both Bruce and Anderson spent a good deal of time at the Connellans' place, helping out with yard work, doing other chores, and eating home-cooked meals for the first time since they left home. They became so close to the Connellans that they started calling them Ma and Pa. The Connellans stayed in touch with both men throughout the war. They even wrote Bruce's parents a letter of congratulations when they learned he had been discharged from the army. Bruce and Anderson's fun in Gladstone came to an end after a month when Company G was ordered back to Rockhampton and replaced by another Company.[42]

In July of 1942, the recently created Japanese 8th fleet landed some 13,000 soldiers near the village of Buna on New Guinea's northern coast. That invasion came just a few weeks before an Allied planned landing in the same area. Both sides hoped to use Buna as the location for an airfield, but the Japanese got there first. From Buna Japanese planes would be able to more effectively bomb Australia's northern coast, support the Japanese army as it made its assault on the New Guinea town of Port Moresby, which was very near Australia itself, and be able to threaten Allied ships headed for Australia. This was something the Allies could not allow. The battle for New Guinea had begun. In December the men of Company G, including Bruce, Anderson, and Baird, were deployed to New Guinea where they would be the first elements of the 41st Division to confront the Japanese army.[43] When the 163rd boarded ships in Gladstone Harbor bound for Port Moresby, New Guinea, June and Dorothy went to the Gladstone docks to see Bruce and Anderson off.[44]

CHAPTER 3

New Guinea, Buna–Sanananda

December 25, 1942–February 1, 1943

While Bruce, Anderson, and Baird endured the training regimen and alternately enjoyed their time in Gladstone, major events of the war in the Pacific took place elsewhere. The devastating blow the Japanese had dealt the United States at Pearl Harbor had not bought them enough time to accomplish their goals. Competing forces in the Japanese Military Command vied for implementation of their separate plans and the equipment and supplies needed to accomplish them. This divided Japanese resources and prevented the Japanese from moving as quickly as they might have.

Following successful attacks on America's possessions in the mid-Pacific (the Aleutian Islands, Guam, and the Philippines) many powerful people in the Japanese navy wanted to rush into the second phase of their offensive: the conquest of the island of New Guinea from which they could launch attacks against Australia and a possible invasion. The Japanese Imperial Army objected to what they felt were overly ambitious plans and convinced the head of the Imperial Navy to settle for a more limited move to the south that involved occupying the northern coast of Papua New Guinea and the Solomon Islands.

Even this limited plan for a southern offensive was put on hold because of Admiral Isoroku Yamamoto's insistence that Japan concentrate its forces on a westward move across the mid-Pacific to further reduce American naval power in Hawaii. As the hero of Japan's attack on Pearl Harbor, Yamamoto's opinion carried great weight with the Japanese War Council and the ships, men, and equipment necessary for the southern offensive were devoted to the attack on Midway.

Several things thwarted and complicated the Japanese plans. First, audacious U.S. bombing raids on Japan itself in February of 1942 convinced the Japanese that they needed to strengthen their outer island defenses. This made at least a limited move south more of a priority. From its large military base at Rabaul, the Japanese army successfully invaded the Island of New Britain which had an excellent natural port. From New Britain they attempted to land an invading army on New Guinea's northern coast at Lae and Salamaua. This invasion was thwarted when U.S. Admiral Chester Nimitz received intelligence warning of the invasion and dispatched dive-bombers launched from the carriers USS *Lexington* and USS *Yorktown* that made landing troops in New Guinea seem too risky.[1] The presence of two U.S. carriers off the northeastern coast of Australia led to the battle of the Coral Sea in May of 1942. The battle was a material victory for Japan, but a strategic victory for the United States. The Japanese navy's failure to destroy or drive off the U.S. Navy further delayed and limited their actions in New Guinea and the Solomon Islands.[2]

The crippling defeat of the Japanese invasion force and the destruction of four Japanese aircraft carriers at the battle of Midway ended Japan's expansion to the west and renewed the importance of offensive action to the south. Only now New Guinea and the Solomon Islands were seen more as a valuable first line of defense against attack instead of bases from which the Japanese could launch attacks on Australia. Japanese forces already occupied the island of Tulagi and Guadalcanal in the Solomon Islands when a Japanese invasion force of 13,000 men landed on New Guinea's northern coast near the village of Buna on July 22. From the beaches of Buna, the Japanese fought their way inland to the Kokoda Trail which led over the Owen Stanley Mountains that divided New Guinea roughly north and south. The Japanese general in charge of the New Guinea invasion planned to cross those mountains and capture the city of Port Moresby on the southern Coast. From Port Moresby Japan might still hope to threaten allied shipping in the Coral Sea and the northern Australian coast. Despite the nightmarish climate and terrain of New Guinea, the Japanese drove New Guinea's Australian defenders over the mountains and to within sight of the lights of Port Moresby. Allied command sent the battle-hardened 7th Australian Division and the untested American 32nd Division to defend Port Moresby. The combined Allied forces launched a counterattack which drove the Japanese away from Port Moresby and back up the Kokoda Trail. When the U.S. Marines landed on Tulagi and Guadalcanal on August 7, 1942, Japanese bombers, tasked with providing air support to the Japanese army fighting on the Kokoda Trail in New Guinea, were redirected to attack U.S. landing ships at Guadalcanal. This would not be the last time that the fighting at Guadalcanal affected the battle for New Guinea and vice versa. The determination of the Japanese to hold New Guinea and Guadalcanal without enough men, ships, or airplanes doomed their defense of both.[3]

After successfully defending southern New Guinea, the Allies fight for control of the island's northern half began in earnest in the fall of 1942. The Australians and the men of the 32nd Division battled the swamps, jungle, muddy mountain trails, dysentery, malaria, and dengue fever in order to attack the Japanese and chase them back over the mountains to their beach defenses around Buna and Gona. The Japanese failure to drive the Americans off Guadalcanal caused their high command to shift 2,000 reinforcements to New Guinea. Those reinforcements arrived just before the Allied assault on Buna and Gona began.

Weeks of fighting did little to force the Japanese out or to destroy their positions at Buna and Gona. General MacArthur, who by this time had moved his headquarters to Port Moresby, grew frustrated with the lack of progress and replaced the commander of the 32nd Division. MacArthur had no clear idea of the difficulties the men of that division faced or how devastating their fight over the mountains had been and neither did General Robert Eichelberger, who MacArthur put in charge of the division. Nevertheless, Eichelberger ordered a renewed assault on the Japanese positions at Buna while the Australians renewed their efforts to take Gona. On December 15, Gona fell to the Australians. Their success put even more pressure on the Americans attacking Buna. Finally, elements of the 32nd Division broke through the Japanese defenses on the beach and the Americans moved into Buna village. Despite the Allied success the Japanese soldiers remaining in the Buna—Gona area seemed committed to fighting to the last man. Japanese fanaticism frustrated the Australians and the Americans and their willingness to fight on at any cost horrified the Allies.

Though General MacArthur declared victory in Buna and Gona on January 8, 1943, it would be several weeks before allied forces cleared all the Japanese from the area. Allied military analysts believed that even after the fall of Buna the Japanese still had a fighting force of some 7,000 men defending nearby Sanananda Point and more beyond the Kumusi River up the New Guinea coast to the west, where they had retreated after the initial American attack on Gona.[4] As the battles for Buna and Gona ground on, MacArthur decided to commit more men to the fight. He ordered the 163rd Regiment to New Guinea and assigned the regiment the task of clearing the Japanese from the Soputa–Sanananda Road and the trails leading to and from it.

On Christmas Day 1942, the 163rd Regimental Combat Team (consisting of the 163rd Infantry Regiment, elements of the 41st Signal Company, the 41st Quartermaster Company, the 116th Engineer Battalion, and the 641st Tank Destroyer Battalion) boarded ships from Gladstone, Australia and headed for Port Moresby on New Guinea's southern coast. Company G was assigned to a Dutch merchant ship called the *Bonteka*. The captain and the other officers of the ship were Dutch, but the crew were Javanese. Jack Anderson found the trip to be a trying one. For security reasons the men were ordered to stay below decks, which meant they only got fresh air when they went to relieve themselves. That activity proved to be an adventure. The "toilets" were located on the fantail and were just sets of boards with a gap between them that hung out over the water. The men had to squat with one foot on either side of that gap to relieve themselves. Conditions below deck were grim. The cargo areas had been equipped with hammocks but there were no showers and very little fresh water. Because the below-deck areas had not been intended for people, there was no way to effectively circulate fresh air through the area where the men stayed.[5] Company G and the rest of the 163rd spent Christmas 1942 at sea. Their Christmas dinner consisted of "bully beef" (potted meat) with two jawbreaker candies for dessert.[6]

Fortunately, the trip only took two days. The 163rd arrived at Port Moresby, New Guinea on December 27. The regiment's time in Fort Stanley would also be brief. Anderson and the men of Company G made camp near the airstrips from which they would take off a few days later.[7]

The wait at Port Moresby frustrated the men of Company G who, now that they were near the combat area, wanted to get on with it. What several of them got first was dysentery. The men who contracted it spent their days before the trip over the Owen Stanley Mountains wearing only their rain ponchos and carrying shovels with them everywhere they went.[8] They also received some new equipment, ammunition, and training. During a bayonet training Anderson got a wound on his wrist that left a scar, his first, but unofficial, wound of the war.[9]

On December 30, the regiment's 1st Battalion crawled into small cargo planes and began crossing the Owen Stanley Mountains that divided New Guinea north and south. The other battalions followed. The planes could only hold a dozen or so men and their equipment and would fly just above the trees through a pass in the mountains during the times that there were no reports of Japanese fighter planes over the pass. The planes could turn around before they reached the pass, but once in the pass they would have to keep going until they reached the other side. The trip only took thirty minutes, but they were thirty very tense minutes.[10] Doyle Bruce, like most of the other men on the small plane he and his equipment had been crammed into, was scared for the whole thirty minutes. Bruce and twelve other men sat on the floor of the plane, one behind the other with their legs stretched out to the sides for the entire flight. Japanese Zeros had been spotted in the area as Bruce's plane entered the pass. The only protection the plane had was a soldier sitting in the open doorway with a Browning Automatic Rifle. They would not stand a chance if spotted by a Japanese fighter plane attacking from above.[11]

Anderson, Bruce, Baird, and the rest of the 2nd Battalion of the 163rd made it through the pass without incident. They landed on a recently constructed airstrip at Dobodura near their first objective on the Soputa–Sanananda Road. Bruce remembered that the men in his plane were ordered to jump out of the plane as it went down the runway so the plane would not have to come to a full stop.[12] During the march Company G passed the wounded and tired soldiers of the 32nd Division and encountered elements of the Australian Army for the first time. Their orderliness and professionalism as well as their toughness impressed Bruce. He thought they were the best soldiers in the world and brave,

Members of the 163rd Regiment on board a transport plane flying them back to Port Moresby, July 1943. Similar small planes had flown the men of the 163rd over to combat in the Buna–Sanananda region in January of 1943. (National Archives)

superb fighting men. He did not think they were tougher or stronger than the Americans, but he thought they were more mentally prepared for combat. Bruce believed that the average Australian soldier could be dropped off in the deepest, densest river bottom in East Texas, and he would walk out with his uniform clean and shiny.[13]

As the highest-ranking man on the hollowed-out old Hudson bomber that flew Bruce Baird and his squad over the mountains, the pilot ordered Baird to sit behind him during the flight so that as soon as the plane landed on the airstrip near Dobodura he could show him where to lead his men and give him instructions. The most important instruction he

received was to move off the airstrip and into the jungle as fast as possible
so that any Japanese fighter plane flying overhead would not see his
men as an attractive target. When the plane landed the pilot pointed to
the trailhead leading to the gathering point for 2nd Battalion and Baird
hurried his men off the plain and into the jungle. He and his men hiked
to Dobodura to join the rest of Company G. Along the way they saw
dozens of Australian men, including wounded, encountered some of
the indigenous people of New Guinea who were acting as porters, and
saw the putrefying bodies of a few dead Japanese soldiers. Company G's
first base camp was located very near an Australian artillery piece which
fired intermittently and made it difficult for the men to sleep during
their first night in a combat zone.[14] Anderson and a dozen other men
boarded what he referred to as a "Boston Bomber"—which was the
nickname for the Douglas Boston A-20 Havoc—for their flight through
the Owen Stanleys. The plane took off and flew as low as possible
toward the entrance to the mountain pass. Reports of a Japanese fighter
plane over the pass forced the plane back to the airstrip at Port Moresby.
Anderson's plane was among the last to land on the pierced metal panels
that had been put down at the Dobodura airstrip.[15] Once all the men of
Company G were on the ground and gathered, they began their march
into the jungle to relieve the 39th Australian Infantry Battalion in the
southernmost Allied position on the road.[16]

The 163rd Regiment's mission was to take control of the Soputa–
Sanananda Road, reduce Japanese defensive positions, and prevent
Japanese soldiers from using the road to escape the interior of New
Guinea to reinforce the Japanese position at Sanananda Point or to be
evacuated to another area. Trails crisscrossed the road at many points along
its length. The most important of which were the Sanananda Road itself
and the Killerton Trail. The Japanese had established defensive positions
all along the road and at trail junctions. These defenses consisted of earth
and log bunkers arranged in a circular or oval pattern on both sides of
the road. They dug slit trenches arranged in a way to both take advantage
of the dense jungle cover and to control fields of fire that covered the
approaches along the road and trails. Their positions were sunk into
the fetid swamp and jungle of New Guinea and surrounded by trip wires

and improvised alarm systems. Snipers hid in trees and Japanese patrols searched the surrounding area for the presence of their enemies.[17]

New Guinea's swamps and jungles made combat hellish. The trails and land over which the Americans moved and on which they set up their own positions flooded at high tide or in heavy rain. The high kunai grass hid enemy machine-gun emplacements and potentially large numbers of Japanese soldiers. Deep mud and water made movement off the trails and through the jungle very difficult. Movement at night proved so dangerous that the men were ordered not to leave their positions for fear of Japanese ambush. It was the rainy season in New Guinea which meant the men and their clothing were almost always wet. In the heat and humidity of the jungle their clothes blackened and rotted. The rate at which the men contracted malaria, dengue fever, and dysentery created a constant problem for troop strength and combat operations.[18]

The arrangement of Japanese and Allied positions along the Sanananda Road was intricate and confusing to both armies. There were small and large defensive perimeters created by both sides, interspersed in leapfrog fashion, with the junction of the road and Killerton Trail held by the Japanese to the south to the Allied force's Musket Perimeter to the north. There were at least three other matching sets of Allied and Japanese positions further along the road to the north. These positions were right on top of one another, but often shielded from view by the New Guinea rainforest.

The Japanese position farthest south along the road was a major obstacle to the Allied objective of seizing control of the road. The Australian 18th Division held the ground south of the Japanese position, but other Allied units had also reached the road to the north of the Japanese where they established Musket Perimeter. The Allied position there forced the Japanese to use the unsecured Killerton Trail to keep their position supplied.

1st Battalion of the 163rd began its relief of the Australians in Musket Perimeter in early January of 1943. The perimeter had been built by the Australians on a piece of ground slightly higher than the swampy jungle floor to reduce the threat of flooding. The perimeter's defenses consisted of inner and outer rings of foxholes with slit trenches, supply dumps, and medical aid stations in the center.[19] To create a perimeter, the men dug

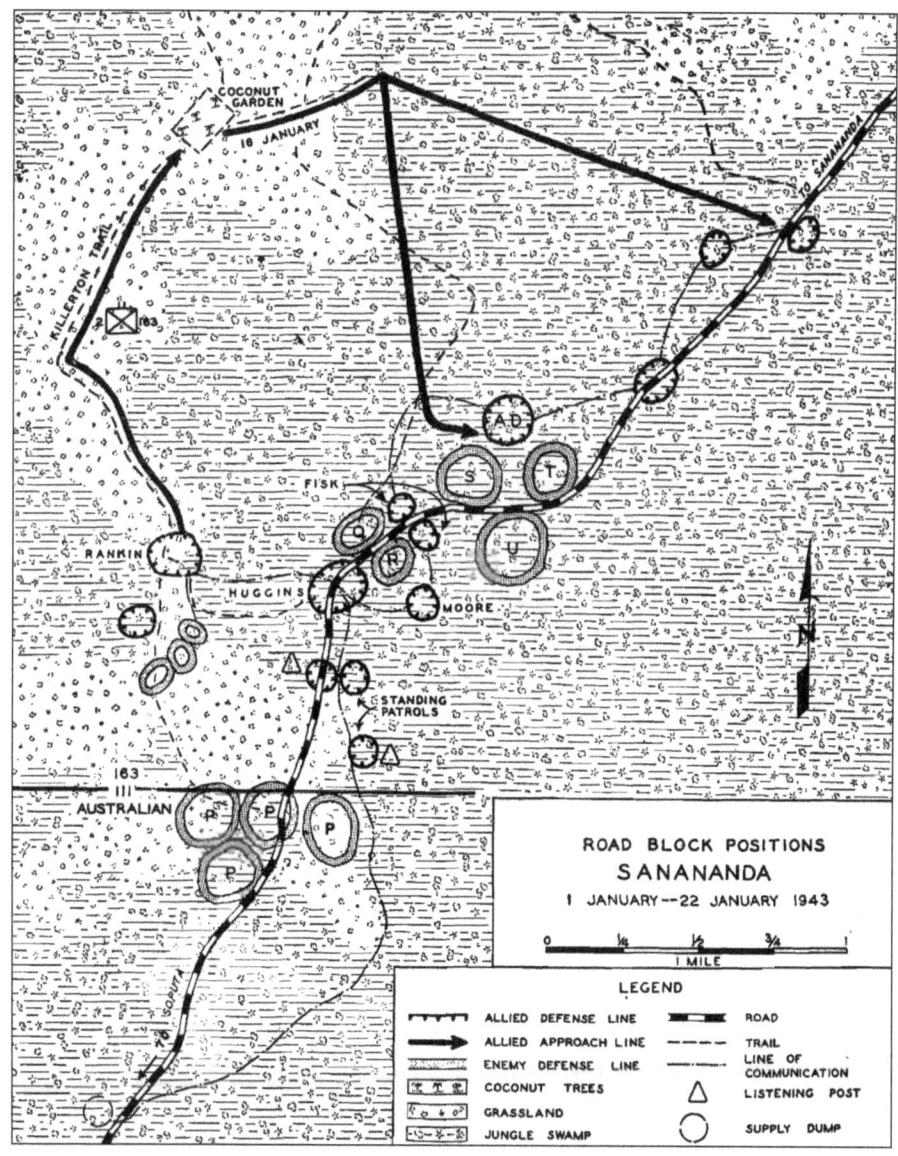

ROAD BLOCK POSITIONS
SANANANDA
1 JANUARY--22 JANUARY 1943

LEGEND

ALLIED DEFENSE LINE		ROAD	
ALLIED APPROACH LINE		TRAIL	
ENEMY DEFENSE LINE		LINE OF COMMUNICATION	
COCONUT TREES		LISTENING POST	
GRASSLAND		SUPPLY DUMP	
JUNGLE SWAMP			

This map shows the position of Allied and Japanese positions along the Sanananda Road and the Killerton Track when 2nd Battalion of the 163rd Infantry took over combat operation in the area. (U.S. Army Center of Military History)

two-man foxholes. The more dangerous the area, the closer together those foxholes were. At night one man in each foxhole was always awake and the men usually took it in one- to two-hour shifts. They made as little noise as possible and never left their hole, not even to relieve themselves, for fear of being shot by other men in other foxholes. During the day sentries posted along trails leading in and out of the area guarded the approaches to the perimeter and the men not on guard duty could stay above ground and relax in the perimeter's interior.[20]

When the men of 1st Battalion took over Musket Perimeter, they found that Japanese snipers had set up firing stations in the trees surrounding their position. The Australians had not taken effective steps to eliminate the threat from these snipers, but the Americans did. During their patrols 1st Battalion found two Japanese positions on either side of the road to the north of Musket Perimeter. These positions were the first true combat targets of the 163rd. The companies of 1st Battalion launched an attack to reduce or destroy them but failed due to the terrain, logistical issues, and the stubbornness of the Japanese soldiers. This action resulted in the 163rd Regiment's first casualties of the war.[21]

On January 7, 2nd Battalion reached Musket Perimeter. Though the danger had been much reduced at the time of Company G's arrival in the perimeter, Japanese tree snipers still posed a danger. The men of the 1st Battalion had developed various methods of eliminating them. They positioned American counter snipers in the trees to fire on Japanese snipers after they shot. They sent out foot patrols guided by scouts who climbed in trees to locate the Japanese shooters. They also brought up a 37mm canon that belonged to the 641st Tank Destroyer company to blast the tops of the trees with grapeshot.[22]

Early in Company G's deployment in New Guinea, Jack Anderson's platoon walked into a tree sniper ambush in a clearing covered by kunai grass. The snipers shot the platoon lieutenant and two other men before the rest of the group could get to cover. The shot that hit the lieutenant first entered his throat, traveled through his chest, and then into his elbow. The other two men received more minor wounds. Anderson and another man got to the lieutenant and began to try to drag him to safety but every time they laid him down to drag him, he would sit up after only a few feet putting himself and his rescuers in danger. Despite that difficulty they managed to get him out of the clearing. They later learned that the bullet had pierced the lieutenant's esophagus and so whenever they laid him flat his airway filled with blood, and he could not breathe. The lieutenant survived but he never returned to Company G or to combat. From this encounter and others, the men learned several lessons about snipers. First, to stick to cover at all times no matter how difficult the terrain. Second, pin the sniper down before trying to rescue any wounded. And finally, never approach a wounded man until the sniper is eliminated, because that is exactly what they want you to do.[23]

Because the 37mm guns were not always available and snipers continued to plague the men of the 163rd throughout the early days of combat in New Guinea, company commanders were forced to try any reasonable solution. One of these potential solutions involved sneaking a squad out of the company perimeter just after nightfall and having them set up a hidden position away from the company where they could watch and launch surprise attacks from behind any enemy snipers who moved in to set up positions in the trees. On one occasion early in Company G's time in combat, Bruce Baird and his squad were chosen for this assignment. They snuck out of camp as soon as it was dark and moved into the tall grass on one side of a trail leading to the Company G perimeter. They dug a large foxhole to offer more concealment and protection and began their vigil. A few hours into their watch, biting ants found their way into the foxhole, but Baird and his men knew that if they got out and moved around in the dark, they would likely be fired on by their own men. After midnight American artillery began to fire on a Japanese position further along the trail so that the shells passed over the place where Baird and his men lay hidden. As the night wore on those shells began to drop closer and closer to their hiding place. To Baird it seemed like the shells might be falling on him and his men before the sun came up. In the morning, as it began to get light, Baird had not seen any Japanese snipers, but he had his men fire some rounds into the treetops before they headed back to the perimeter. This ended Baird's sniper patrol, but the shells that he had worried would begin to fall on his squad continued to creep closer and closer to the perimeter and they did not stop until Company G command was able to contact the artillery group.[24]

Doyle Bruce's first impression of New Guinea was that it was hot. Having grown up in the heat and humidity of East Texas, he adapted quickly but noted that the heat posed a serious health risk to the men from the northern states. According to Bruce, the mosquitoes and biting gnats threatened to "eat the men alive." But when it came down to staying cool or being protected from the bugs, Bruce and the other men chose to stay cool. They discarded the mosquito netting that covered their faces because it was hot and made it difficult to hear. He and the other men of Company G learned that what mattered most in New Guinea was surviving New Guinea and the heat seemed like more of an immediate threat than mosquito-borne diseases. In a few weeks many of them would likely rethink that decision. Early on it became apparent to Bruce that the Japanese were far more adept at jungle fighting than the Americans, who he characterized as almost completely unprepared. The men of the 163rd had to learn on the job. Not infrequently the superior knowledge and skill of the Japanese resulted in lost American lives. For Bruce, the Japanese tree snipers were a worrying example of that.[25]

As a sergeant in command of a nine-man rifle squad, Jack Anderson's first days at Musket Perimeter provided valuable—if terrifying—on-the-job training. The squad trained to fight as three groups of three men. Anderson led one group, a corporal another, and the BAR man led the third. As the squad moved forward, whichever group encountered the enemy would hold their position, allowing the other two groups the freedom to maneuver into attack or defensive positions. When possible, the group led by the BAR man established a position to provide fire support for the other groups, who carried out direct assaults or flanking attacks on the enemy. Coordinating these moves in conjunction with orders from his platoon commander was Anderson's responsibility.

Company G spent several days scouting the area around their perimeter in attempt to locate the Japanese positions as accurately as possible. They often blundered into strongly built fortifications, received enemy fire, backed off, and continued scouting for weaker areas that they could attack. From these actions the Americans learned that the Japanese perimeters consisted of trenches that connected to bunkers and that sometimes small perimeters were connected to one another and had overlapping fields of fire. This arrangement meant that each Japanese perimeter could support another and that men could move in relative safety from one area to another. Under American artillery bombardment or mortar fire, Japanese soldiers could shelter in the bunkers and then move quickly back to their firing positions to meet the Americans' attacks.

The basic tactics used by a rifle squad were mirrored at the platoon, company, and battalion level. The tall kunai grass and the thick jungles of New Guinea meant that the only way to locate the enemy was to send men forward to blunder into Japanese positions. Sometimes the men of Company G could get within a few yards of a Japanese perimeter before being fired on. Once located and marked by the patrols, the enemy positions could be bombarded by mortars and field artillery before an infantry assault took place. American commanders avoided ordering assaults on unshelled positions when possible to keep casualties low while the men learned their jobs.[26]

Despite some initial mistakes, Anderson felt that his commanding officers were among the best in the army. The 2nd Battalion of the 163rd Infantry was under the command of Major (later Colonel) Walter R. Rankin. During the fighting along the Sanananda Road, the 2nd would be the most mobile of the regiment's three battalions. Its ability to move quickly through the jungle and carry out its missions effectively earned it the nickname "Rankin's Racers," or sometimes "Rankin's Rangers." Anderson thought Rankin very intelligent and credited him with the ability to plan for most combat situations before they happened. His platoon leader, Lieutenant Arthur "Buck" Braman, dealt patiently with the stubborn and outspoken Anderson and even listened to his ideas from time to time. Company commander Captain William "Wild Bill" Benson was tough, hot headed, and sometimes foolish but he almost always made the right decisions and cared deeply about the men of Company G.[27]

After taking over the positions at Musket Perimeter, the 2nd Battalion's first mission involved providing support for the 1st Battalion in its failed attempt to take the two Japanese positions located to the north along the road. This set back led to the development of more elaborate Allied plans for eliminating Japanese forces in the interior of New Guinea and preventing their escape.

In phase one of this operation, 1st Battalion would hold Musket Perimeter on the Sanananda Road, while 2nd Battalion marched west through the jungle to the Killerton Track where they would establish a defensive position. When all was in place, the 18th Australian Infantry, located south of the Japanese position, would attack catching the Japanese between themselves and Americans who controlled the only two reasonable routes of retreat.

On January 9, Company G led the 2nd Battalion move to the west of Musket Perimeter to establish a new perimeter on the Killerton Track. The Killerton Track was a wide corridor through the jungle that ran along raised land with two-foot-high berms built along its edges to prevent flooding. These precautions kept the track free of water under most conditions, but it created an ideal field of fire for machine guns and mortars. The likelihood of meeting Japanese patrols and outposts along the way was high, but the men of Company G had been warned not to fire their weapons until the battalion reached its objective, to avoid alerting the enemy to their movement. Scouts from 1st Platoon accompanied by company commander Captain Benson and Battalion commander Major Rankin took the point followed by the rest of 1st Platoon, and the remainders of Company G, F, H, and E, in that order. The swampy terrain of the jungle made movement difficult. In some places the mud and muck were only ankle-deep, but in others the men sank up to their thighs. The heat and humidity of the jungle made the air close and the tall kunai grass that covered the swamp cut visibility to almost zero.[28] When 2nd Battalion moved west from Musket Perimeter to establish the "roadblock" on the Killerton Track, Bruce was near the front of the column. His main memories were of kunai grass six feet high or more and swamp water that sometimes came up to his chest.[29]

When Company G reached the track, Captain Benson deployed 1st and 3rd Platoons in the angle where the trail the company had been following connected to the Killerton Track to provide cover for the rest of the company against enemy attacks from the south. Benson then sent one squad from 1st Platoon north along the track to watch for Japanese soldiers coming from the north. With these units in place, Benson ordered 2nd Platoon and part of the weapons platoon to cross the wide-open space of the track and set up a defensive position on the far side. The jungle around Company G remained quiet as the crossing began.

But just as 2nd Platoon and the men from the weapons platoon made it across, two Japanese soldiers were spotted coming along the track from the south and one of the company sergeants in a forward position shot and killed them both. Immediately a Japanese machine gun hidden behind a log that lay across the track, opened up and Japanese mortars began to fall on the area occupied by Company G. Japanese snipers took to the trees from which they could clearly see the outlines of the American GIs who lay prone in the kunai grass.[30] Bruce was among those in the weapons platoon that company commander Benson sent across and, as a result, he was one of the ones trapped on the far side of the track when the Japanese opened fire on Company G.[31]

Four men from Company G were killed in the initial burst of Japanese rifle, machine gun, and mortar fire. As the attack continued, seven more men were wounded. Considering that a company consisted of around 120 men, Company G had sustained an almost ten percent casualty rate in the first few minutes it was in combat. In addition to the dead and wounded, Company G had been split in half by the Japanese attack with elements on both sides of the Killerton Track in defensive positions facing an enemy force of unknown strength. The men of Company G returned fire the best they could and waited for the rest of 2nd Battalion to take action to help them.

Major Rankin attempted to reinforce the Company G men on the far side of the track by having Company F cross the track a little further up the trail, but heavy fire from the Japanese made this impossible. Rankin's next move was to have Companies E, F, and H move through the jungle alongside the track to a slightly elevated spot where they created a defensive perimeter. In New Guinea, defensive positions offered only limited protection because if the men dug their foxholes or trenches too deeply, they filled with water. Unwilling to suffer the high casualties that would result from a frontal assault on the Japanese position and unsure of the enemy location and strength, Rankin had a man climb a tall tree so he could see and report the coordinates of the Japanese machine gun. This information was passed on to the GIs holding Musket Perimeter where a section of 81mm mortars used the coordinates to rain shells down on the Japanese position.[32] The 60mm mortars of Company G's weapons platoon joined in the bombardment. Bruce and his mortar crew played their part in the bombardment of the Japanese position that would eventually knock out the Japanese machine gun that had stymied 2nd Battalion's progress.[33]

Still pinned on either side of the Killerton Track by Japanese rifle and mortar fire, Company G hunkered down in the swamp to spend an anxious and wet night in enemy territory. In the morning, Captain Benson ordered men on both sides of the track to begin digging a trench across its width as a way of providing cover to the men on the far side as they crossed the track and rejoined the rest of the company. To avoid being killed by snipers the men had to dig while lying prone. Bruce helped dig the trench across the track that reunited Company G. He remembered throwing shovels full of dirt in the air so that the men coming from the other direction knew where their half of the trench was and could dig to meet them.[34] It was tough work in the heat and humidity of the New Guinea rainforest, but once completed the company was reunited and Benson was able to properly deploy his men along the edge of the track and bring up a heavy machine gun to cover the approach to 2nd Battalion's position. Company G had experienced significant losses, but they played an important role in helping 2nd Battalion achieve its objective of cutting off a means of escape for the Japanese position farthest south along the Sanananda Road.[35]

Despite these difficulties and losses, by January 12, 2nd Battalion had reached and established a strong defensive position on the Killerton Track and the Australians launched their attack on the Japanese stronghold. That attack failed, but on January 14, a 163rd Regiment patrol captured a sick Japanese soldier who informed them that the Japanese commander had ordered all the remaining able-bodied men to evacuate their position and try to work their way to the coast. The sick and wounded were left behind to slow the Allied advance.[36]

To prevent these men from reinforcing the Japanese at Sanananda Point and otherwise escaping, General Vasey's Australian division and the 2nd Battalion of the 163rd began a coordinated attack on the Japanese position. The 2nd Battalion attacked down the Killerton Track moving from north to south while the Australian division attacked the Japanese position directly moving from south to north.[37]

Company E and G were chosen to lead 2nd Battalion's southward thrust down the Killerton Track. Scouts advanced ahead of both companies through newly abandoned Japanese bunkers and trenches without finding a living Japanese soldier and even made visual contact with advanced elements of the Australian division. But when Company G's 3rd Platoon led a move in force through that same area, they came under heavy fire from tree snipers and a group of Japanese soldiers who had sheltered in a low trench hidden in the underbrush. The fighting was close and deadly. A private named Otis Belin jumped into an abandoned Japanese foxhole and began to return fire. He was so close to the Japanese position that when they threw grenades into his hole, he had time to throw the grenades back before they detonated. Company G concentrated its fire on the Japanese trench, killing twenty enemy soldiers. It then pushed through the enemy position and linked up with the main body of the Australian infantry. This combined action broke the Japanese defense, inflicted heavy casualties, and destroyed their southernmost defensive position.[38]

The Japanese position at the southern end of the Sanananda Road had been eliminated but both the Australians and the Americans had other missions to accomplish. The Australian division moved through the men of 2nd Battalion and up the Killerton Track to envelop the Japanese position on the coast. 2nd Battalion followed them up the track to a clearing known as Coconut Grove and then cut east along another trail in an attempt to reach the Sanananda Road at a point north of the Japanese perimeter to the north of Musket Perimeter. The 163rd Regiment's 1st Battalion had renewed its attack and it was hoped that 2nd Battalion could arrive in time to envelop that position and help destroy it.[39]

On January 15, with Company G in the lead, 2nd Battalion began its trek back to the Sanananda Road on an unknown trail. As Company G moved up the Killerton Track the men of learned to love and trust the native people of New Guinea who the Americans called "Angels." The "Angels" were vital to the success of 2nd Battalion and all the Allied forces that fought in Papua New Guinea. The "Angels" served as porters, following each company with equipment, food, and lifesaving supplies. Bruce also revered the "Angels" because they were the only means of evacuating the wounded men of the company. Because most

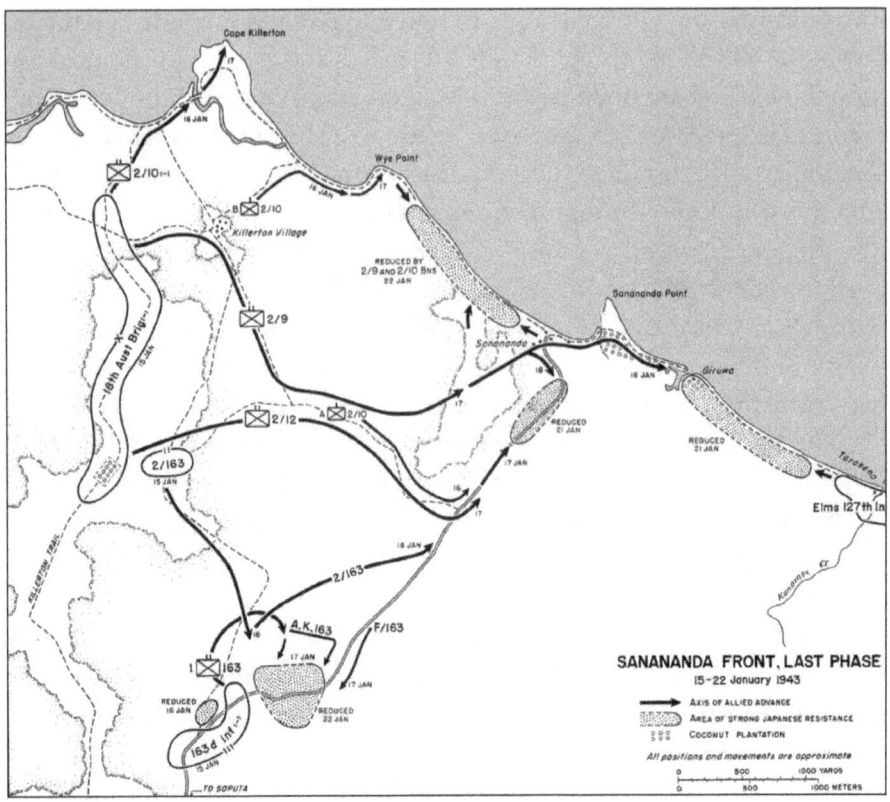

This map shows the movement of the 2nd Battalion of the 163rd Infantry after the reduction of the Japanese position on the Killerton Track. (U.S. Army Center of Military History)

of the actions in which Company G engaged were small-group actions, there were not enough men to evacuate the wounded to a medical aid station. The wounded were either left behind until later or continued on with the company as best they could. But, with the "Angels" following along, wounded men could be carried to the rear for medical attention.[40] Both the Japanese and the Americans conscripted the native people of New Guinea to provide them logistical support, but it was clear that the "Angels" preferred the Americans and the Australians. It was evident that the Japanese had treated these people badly. If tasked to carry litters with wounded Americans, the "Angels" exercised extreme care and caution, not wanting to cause the injured men any more pain. They worked in teams of four or eight to carry the litters on which wounded Americans lay.

Indigenous New Guinea men, who the Americans called "Angels," carry a wounded GI on an improvised litter. Note that four men carry the litter and another four stand by to relieve them when they get tired. (National Archives)

Their experience at walking on the narrow paths through the jungle allowed them to walk two abreast with the litter behind them in places Americans found it difficult to walk in single files. They often carried the litters with their arms extended above their heads to act as shock absorbers to cushion the ride for wounded Americans. But, if given the job of transporting wounded Japanese, the same people would often just dump the wounded in the swamp and leave them to die. Though the Americans appreciated the "Angels"'s work as porters, it was as hospital workers that the "Angels" earned their nickname. The native men of New Guinea were devoted, gentle, and selfless nurses to the sick and wounded Americans.[41]

The 2nd Battalion lived up to its nickname of Rankin's Racers moving quickly through the jungle while eliminating small pockets of Japanese soldiers. The fact that the trail they were following ended 800 yards from the Sanananda Road did not slow them down.[42] Even the men from the heavy weapons platoons and antitank companies kept up the pace despite having to carry all their heavy equipment in their arms or on their backs. In the early days of the fighting around Sanananda infantry companies went into combat with only what they could carry. Because everything the men needed had to be flown in by small planes from the other side of the Owen Stanley Mountains, resupply was difficult and slow.[43] Company G men hacked their way through the jungle and came out on Sanananda Road just when and where they were supposed to. They immediately moved in for the kill, attacking from the rear of the Japanese position. Many Japanese soldiers died in their bunkers when men from Company G threw grenades in through the rear entrances. While 2nd Battalion made its way through the jungle north of Musket Perimeter, 1st Battalion renewed its assault on the positions to its north, thus allowing elements of 1st and 2nd Battalion to envelop and reduce the Japanese position caught between them.

After this brief fight, 2nd Battalion contacted 1st Battalion and continued the move north along the Sanananda Road with 2nd Battalion's Company F in the lead. After a few hundred yards, Company F ran into a small Japanese position along the road that put up stiff resistance. Captain Benson ordered Company G men to take to the jungle once again to encircle the Japanese position. The plan was to move one hundred yards north and then fall on the Japanese from the rear in a similar tactic they had used to reduce the Japanese position earlier in the day. This move took Company G into an unexpected fight.

As the Battalion moved through the jungle, forward scouts from Company G surprised and killed a lone Japanese sentry in a bunker on the edge of a clearing. When men from 3rd Platoon moved into the clearing, they found native-style thatched huts raised on piers several feet off the ground displaying the symbols of a medical facility. To Captain Benson, who had already developed a deep mistrust of the Japanese, it looked like an ideal place for an ambush, so he deployed his men in an attack formation and sent his scouts forward. Armed Japanese soldiers fired on the company's advance men, wounding two and, from Benson and the men of Company G's point of view, forfeiting the right to be treated as a non-combatant medical facility. Benson ordered his 3rd Platoon into the clearing and the "Hospital Fight" was on.

The men in 3rd Platoon drew heavy rifle, machine-gun, and mortar fire as they advanced. Company G responded with intense fire from all the weapons at its disposal. Rifle and mortar fire flattened the hut which held the Japanese machine gun. Then Company G knocked out the Japanese mortar and its crew. With these two hazards eliminated, all the platoons from Company G began moving through the clearing, killing Japanese riflemen as they went. As the Americans entered the remaining shacks, Japanese soldiers in hiding opened fire and Japanese wounded began to detonate grenades to kill themselves and, in the process, take out as many Americans as possible. Faced with these tactics, the men of Company G adopted a policy of shooting every Japanese soldier they saw, whether they were living or appeared to be wounded or dead. In this way the company cleared the area and killed an unknown number of Japanese soldiers.[44]

In his account of the "Hospital Fight," Doyle Bruce emphasized that the Japanese opened fire from the hospital building in the clearing first and that this meant that Company G was free to attack the hospital which was harboring able-bodied enemy soldiers. The weapons platoon, as they often did, fought as a rifle platoon, so he was among the groups of GIs that moved through the clearing and the hospital buildings. After the first few wounded Japanese dropped grenades in an attempt to kill Americans, Bruce, like the other men of Company G, shot the sick, the wounded, the healthy, and the dead to ensure his own safety and that of his comrades. He summed up the event succinctly, explaining that they cleared out a hospital and did not take any prisoners.[45]

Bruce Baird missed the "Hospital Fight" due to illness. Like many of the men of Company G, and in fact many of the men of the U.S. military in New Guinea, he contracted malaria. Following Company G's actions along the Killerton Track he became too weak to carry his equipment and was left behind in an area that served as a temporary field hospital. The next day he had to choose between being evacuated to an actual field hospital behind the lines or rejoining Company G. He walked out of the medical station and rejoined the company the next day. To Baird the men seemed shaken and regretful by what they had seen and done during the "Hospital Fight."[46]

When news of the hospital fight reached Japanese propagandist Tokyo Rose, she labeled the entire 41st Division "The Bloody Butchers of Sanananda." The men of the 163rd heard her broadcast weeks later while recuperating from the fighting in New Guinea and liked the nickname so much that they began referring to themselves as "MacArthur's Bloody Butchers" until the division earned the more official nickname of "Jungleers."[47] The 41st Division had several nicknames over the course of the war. They were called "The Sunset Division" for the distinctive setting sun patch the men war on their arms and later "The Jungleers" for their expertise in jungle fighting that they earned through hard experience in New Guinea. But many of the men of the 163rd liked the nickname inspired by Tokyo Rose the best.[48]

After the "Hospital Fight" Company G returned to the Sanananda Road and set up a military-style "roadblock" to prevent Japanese soldiers still trapped inland from moving up the road to the Japanese position at Sanananda Point on the coast. This position came under attack from retreating Japanese soldiers on six consecutive nights. In the first of these attacks, the members of 3rd Platoon were thought lost, though all survived. To limit American casualties and more efficiently kill the retreating Japanese, 3rd Platoon's commander, Lieutenant Braman devised a method for ambushing them. He left a few men out on the road in a forward position to alert the platoon to the presence of the enemy while most of the platoon hid in the jungle off the side of the road. When Japanese soldiers coming along the road ran into the Americans they would take to the jungle where they would walk into the American ambush. This tactic was brutally effective. In just one day they killed thirteen of fourteen Japanese soldiers and on another they were attacked by twenty Japanese troops and killed them all.[49]

Bruce Baird's platoon took a turn manning the road ambush. To maintain the secrecy of their position the men had to sleep in the jungle off the raised road, but the low, swampy land of the jungle flooded at night. To stay dry the men built simple sleeping platforms out of tree branches to raise them above the soggy ground. On one of the nights that Baird's platoon manned the ambush he and the others began to hear the cracking of wood followed by a splash that was followed by

Emaciated Japanese prisoners being escorted to headquarters by U.S. soldiers in the Sanananda region in January or February 1943. (National Archives)

curses as, one by one, some of the more shoddily built sleeping platforms collapsed, depositing their occupants in swamp water. Though their orders were to maintain silence, the men who stayed dry began to laugh as more men wound up in the swamp. Another incident during their time on ambush proved more important, if less amusing. As a rule, Baird's platoon killed any Japanese soldier they saw coming down the road. Even during daylight hours, taking a Japanese soldier prisoner was rare, though they could improve their odds by presenting themselves unarmed. Members of one such group who tried to surrender to Baird's squad were captured and sent to headquarters. Baird later learned that they were Koreans who had been captured by the Japanese and forced to work as servants to Japanese officers. From that point on the men of the 163rd learned to spot the facial characteristics of Koreans so they could be captured and provide information to the American military intelligence.[50]

Life in combat offered few sources of comfort for the men of Company G. They learned to discard anything that made their heavy packs a little lighter. This included bulky and useless gas masks as well as blankets and extra clothes that soaked up water and became heavy. They did keep extra socks which they tried to keep dry so that they could change out of their wet socks at night. The men learned that underwear also got wet and led to painful chafing and rashes, so they did not wear underwear under their uniforms. Instead, they wore the underwear as shorts when they got breaks from the fighting and were in more secure areas. Water collected in their helmets provided the only source of hygiene or sanitation, but most of the men chose not to shave and did not worry about bathing in combat areas. For drinking water, they dug holes in the sandy soil and waited for it to fill with water which they gathered in their canteens and to which they then added chlorine tabs. Despite that precaution, dysentery became a problem for a number of the men. The men almost never had hot food while in combat areas unless they warmed their rations themselves using a can of jellified gasoline. Their rations were a mix of canned foods, crackers, or melt-proof chocolate provided by the Australian or American armies. The American rations often included Spam and the Australian canned mutton or "bully beef" that the men often found to be inedible. For breakfast the men soaked the hard tack in water overnight and then poured powdered milk over it and heated it, if they could, to make a kind of porridge. For some men the quality of food, illness, exhaustion, and stress caused them to refuse to eat at all and the other men of the company had to watch them closely and encourage them to eat.[51] In an attempt to supplement their diet with fresh meat, Doyle Bruce and some other men killed and cooked one of the wild hogs that populated the New Guinea jungle. Only afterwards did they realize that the hog might have been feasting on the corpses of dead Japanese soldiers. They did not hunt hogs again.[52]

The last Japanese position on the Sanananda Road was destroyed on January 22, but pockets of Japanese soldiers continued to pose a threat to the men of Company G. On January 24 two Japanese soldiers surrendered to men from Company G claiming they were Buddhist monks and offered to lead the Americans to a group of twenty-six Japanese soldiers hidden in the jungle who wanted to surrender. The next day two platoons from Company G moved into the jungle about 400 yards off the road in search of those wishing to surrender. They came upon a hidden Japanese position whose bunkers and trenches contained the bodies of Japanese soldiers who had died of wounds, starvation, or disease. There were also two live Japanese soldiers, one of whom tried to run and was cut down by American rifle fire. Then, a hidden Japanese rifleman opened fire on the Americans, wounding two. Captain Benson decided his men were in too much danger to continue and ordered a return to their position on the Sanananda Road. During this maneuver, the company's rear guard came under fire again and one man was killed.[53]

On another occasion, Bruce Baird's platoon received orders to retrieve the bodies of two American GIs killed near a Japanese medical facility in the jungle. They had been caught in an ambush when some surrendering Japanese soldiers changed their minds. When Baird and his platoon reached the area, they found the bodies of the two Americans and two dead Japanese nearby. To make sure there were no more enemy soldiers in the area Baird and a few other men entered the structure that held the Japanese medical station. They walked into a nightmare. The building contained the corpses of many Japanese soldiers in various states of decay. Some of the dead had apparently starved to death, some had killed themselves, and some had killed one another. Baird and the others removed the American bodies and returned to camp without discussing what they had seen.[54]

When major combat missions along the Sanananda Road came to an end Company G took over an Australian position along the beaches at Sanananda Point. Here they got the chance to wash their clothes and bathe in the ocean. The Australians had left behind supplies of canned vegetables and fruit as well as cocoa and other sweets that improved the men's diets and morale.[55] The relative ease of their time on the beach would not last long; Company G had one more combat mission to complete before their fight in New Guinea was over.

The Allied victory at Sanananda eliminated the threat of a land based Japanese assault on Port Moresby and therefore reduced the likelihood of serious attacks on, or a Japanese invasion of, Australia itself. The 163rd

Regiment of the 41st bore most of the responsibility for the combat that took place along the Sanananda Road. The regiment counted more than 1400 Japanese killed and boasted of having captured more Japanese equipment than any other Allied unit at that time. The losses they inflicted on the Japanese were disproportionate to their own, but the men of the 163rd had been ravaged by disease, injury, dehydration, heat, and an implacable enemy that would fight almost to the last man.[56]

Company G and its officers performed well in their first combat assignment. They successfully met all their objectives and proved they could move and fight effectively under adverse conditions with limited direct contact with regimental and division command. They survived the nightmare of fighting in the disease-ridden swamps and rainforests of New Guinea where, in addition to fighting the Japanese, they had to battle deadly and debilitating diseases. Like most of the men of Company G, Bruce, Anderson, and Baird contracted malaria while fighting in New Guinea and suffered with it for the remainder of the war and for years afterward. Due to manpower shortages, serious illness did not automatically excuse a soldier from his duties. Anderson went on patrol with high fevers and then stood guard at night with little to relieve his symptoms other than handfuls of aspirin and quinine tablets. As sick as malaria made him, Anderson knew that there were worse diseases a soldier could get in New Guinea. "Black Water Fever" had symptoms similar to malaria, but it did not respond to aspirin or quinine. Those who got it suffered without relief and almost always died. The few men who did survive never fully recovered physically or mentally.[57]

As the American GIs developed a love for the "Angels," they developed a deep and violent hatred for the Japanese soldiers. The fanaticism, and what the Americans considered immoral tactics of the Japanese soldiers, earned their antipathy within a few days of combat. For the American infantrymen, like those of Company G, there were only two goals: accomplish the mission, and survive. The unwillingness of the Japanese to surrender when beaten earned the Americans' hatred. After being the victims of Japanese suicide attacks carried out by sick, wounded, and surrendering Japanese soldiers, the American GIs had little sympathy for their suffering. They looked the other way at reports that the Australians routinely loaded Japanese prisoners onto planes and then threw them out at a great height.[58] The Americans' loathing of the Japanese increased when they discovered that starving Japanese soldiers had cannibalized the corpses of U.S. soldiers.[59] In the early days of fighting along the Sanananda Road, the Americans found evidence of this cannibalism in Japanese positions that they overran. Most notably, the body of Lieutenant Fisk, who was one of the first members of the 163rd to die in combat, was discovered tied to a lattice with his legs removed—presumably eaten by the Japanese.[60]

Though Baird managed to feel sympathy for the Japanese soldiers that he had seen die of starvation, suicide, in combat, or at the hands of their own comrades, Bruce, like many of the GIs who fought in New Guinea and elsewhere in the Pacific, observed things about Japanese soldiers that engendered quite different emotions. One of the curious things he learned fighting in New Guinea was that Japanese soldiers usually fell backwards after being shot while Americans fell forward. Bruce attributed this to the difference in size between the Japanese and Americans and the fact that the American rifles fired a more powerful and higher-caliber round.[61] It was an observation that gives some insight into the number of dead soldiers of both armies that he had seen. He believed the Japanese fanaticism made them bad soldiers and felt their willingness, almost eagerness, to die for their emperor accounted for this weakness. Bruce's participation in the "Hospital Fight" did nothing to change that opinion and his firsthand witnessing of evidence that Japanese soldiers had cannibalized dead Americans likely sealed it. Assigned to bury the bodies of dead GIs found in Japanese positions, Bruce saw firsthand how the Japanese had butchered the bodies by cutting out their livers and the muscles from their legs. He personally saw human remains in the cooking pots of the Japanese.[62]

Over the course of the war, both the Americans and the Japanese came to consider each other to be barely human savages capable of any act of barbarism. At the very least, Bruce agreed with the unofficial U.S. policy regarding Japanese prisoners in New Guinea; with few men to guard them and limited supplies of food, unless specifically ordered to send Japanese prisoners to HQ for questioning, they simply killed them. To Bruce this was fair because he knew the Japanese did not take prisoners either.[63]

Jack Anderson's combat experience taught him that despite the shortage of supplies and lack of air support during the fighting in the Sanananda area, the American soldiers had a technological advantage. The Garand M1 rifle with its eight-round clip and semi-automatic function gave the American GI more firepower than the Japanese soldiers armed with a five-shot bolt-action rifle. In his experience the .30 caliber, high-powered round fired by the M1 more often passed through enemy soldiers, creating multiple wounds, as opposed to the .25 caliber round fired by the Japanese rifle. The grenades used by the Japanese, which were armed by striking them on the helmet, made an identifiable noise that alerted the Americans that grenades were incoming, often giving them time to throw them back before they detonated. He also felt the lightweight Japanese "knee mortar" was no match for the 60mm mortar carried by the weapons platoon of every American infantry company.[64] As the war in the Pacific went on and the United States geared up for military manufacturing the discrepancy in weapons, quality and number, would give the American military an increasing advantage.

CHAPTER 4

The Kumusi River Patrol

February 1, 1943–February 14, 1943

The 41st Division distinguished itself during the Buna–Sanananda Campaign, killing hundreds of enemy soldiers and capturing more enemy equipment than any other Allied force of its size in the Pacific at that time. After January 22, most of the 163rd Regiment spent time on patrol and in mopping up missions while other elements of the 41st Division began to arrive in New Guinea and take on a larger share of the work. As the other battalions and companies of the 163rd moved into rear areas for rest and relaxation the men of 2nd Battalion's Company G were given a new combat assignment.[1]

Company G received orders to travel northwest along the coast of New Guinea from their position on the beach near Sanananda Point to cut off a Japanese route of escape from the interior of the island. Army intelligence reported that around 200 Japanese soldiers had raided native villages for supplies and were planning to float down the Kumusi River to a rallying point on the beach from which they could be evacuated.[2]

For Doyle Bruce the Kumusi River patrol was a grueling, green nightmare. When he recalled the patrol decades later, he talked about the patrol lasting for only five or six days when in reality it was fourteen days. He, like many other members of Company G, had contracted malaria, but because his fever never reached 103 degrees, he was not taken off the line. He soldiered on through the days in a near delirium and slept on piles of sticks to stay dry with no source of comfort at night.[3] Like Bruce, Anderson suffered with severe malaria during the Kumusi River patrol and the heat, humidity, mosquitos, lack of fresh water, and shortage of food added to his pain and discomfort.[4]

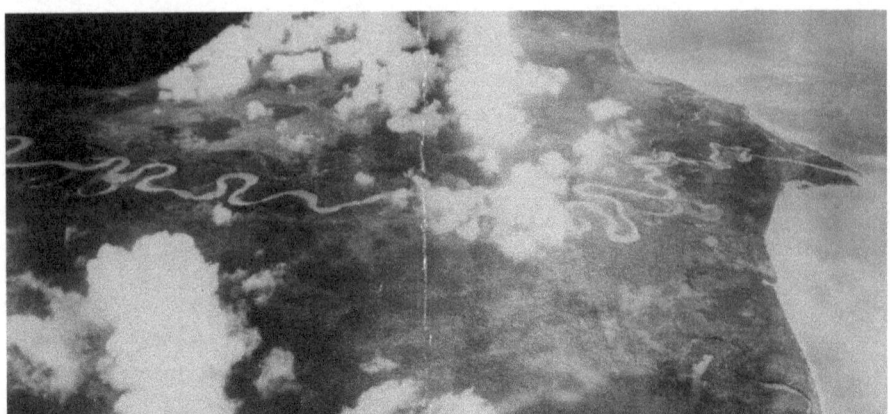

Aerial view of the Kumusi River in Papua New Guinea. Japanese soldiers used the river as an escape route from the interior of the island. (National Archives)

During the patrol Company G operated alone and at some distance from the rest of the 163rd Regiment and the main body of Allied forces at Sanananda. This added an extra layer of danger because of the difficulty of evacuating and treating the wounded. Because they did not carry stretchers while on small group scouting missions and because their numbers were limited, the men of Company G left their wounded comrades on the side of the trail to wait for medics or for others to come and evacuate them after the fire fight stopped. Even when medics arrived they could only provide basic care to the wounded who often had to wait hours before they could be evacuated to hospital facilities near Buna. As a result, some of the wounded men who might have survived died of their wounds instead.[5]

On February 1, 1943, Company G, under the command of Captain "Wild Bill" Benson, set out on a twenty-two-mile hike along beaches, across rivers, and through dense jungle in an effort to cut off the Japanese route of escape. The first obstacle the company faced was Killerton Bay itself. Benson decided the best way to overcome that obstacle was to go right through it. He ordered the eighty-eight men of Company G who were fit for duty, the dozen men from 2nd Battalion Headquarters, two radio men, two medics, a six-man medical team, and more than 200 native carriers to wade across the mile width of the bay. The coral-bottomed bay offered solid footing and was only waist deep in most places, but occasionally men got stuck in the mud on the bottom or stepped off into deeper water with a full pack and full uniform, which meant that some of them had to be rescued.[6] Bruce, at over six feet in height, was in no danger, but he had to save a shorter member of the company from drowning and from then on that soldier thanked Bruce whenever he saw him.[7]

Company G made camp on the far side of the bay where they discovered evidence of the recent presence of enemy soldiers in the form of discarded food containers. On the morning of February 2, Company G hiked for three hours to Sebari village where they were joined by a platoon from Company G of the 186th Regiment. The 186th was one of the other two regiments that made up the 41st Division, but the men of its Company G platoon, whose commander was a First Lieutenant named Carstner, had no combat experience. By comparison, the men of the 163rd Company G were hardened veterans. Carstner reported that his men had made contact with a Japanese position 600 yards farther into the jungle. Benson led his force of nearly 150 men toward the south bank of the Kombela River, sending a scouting party out in front of the main body of his force. The scouts reported no signs of the enemy between Company G and the south bank of the river from where it emptied into the sea to a depth of several hundred yards inland. Company G arrived at the deep and fast-moving Kombela River a short time later and observed what they believed to be a Japanese position across the river, just inside the edge of the jungle. The geography favored the Japanese. Not only was the river between the Americans and their position largely concealed by jungle, but there was also an open sand flat more than sixty yards wide on their side of the river that the GIs would have to cross. Unlike most of the rivers the company encountered, the Kombela could not be waded.

Benson's plan of attack involved sending a three-man patrol across the river on an improvised raft, while another team brought up an abandoned Japanese assault boat the company had found on the beach. Benson planned to use the Japanese boat to ferry the rest of the company and its equipment across the river. Sergeant Ronald Bretzke, Private William Ramsey, and an Australian Warrant Officer named Dixon (attached to

Benson's command to act as a liaison with the native carriers) volunteered to cross the river as scouts. A team of men under the direction of Corporal Arthur Sahs were given the task of bringing the assault boat along the coast and getting it into position.

The three men crossed the river under the watchful eyes of the rest of Benson's force which was strung out in the jungle along the south bank of the river and began a patrol inland from the beach. Just steps inside the edge of the jungle, they found five Japanese soldiers and opened fire. Both Bretzke and Ramsey put their men down and then the patrol turned and ran for the beach and the river. Machine-gun fire forced the three men down on the sand. When Bretzke raised up to return fire, he was hit and killed. The two remaining members of the patrol rolled down the beach to the river. There they stripped off their clothes and swam out one hundred yards to sea before swimming back to Company G's position.[8] Bretzke was a close friend of Anderson and Anderson would later help bury his body. He would not be the only friend of Anderson's to die while on the Kumusi patrol.[9]

Japanese machine-gun fire also poured into Company G's position from the jungle on the far side of the river. Benson sent two BAR men further into the jungle to a position from which they could return fire on the Japanese machine gun. In the meantime, the Japanese also opened up with machine-gun fire and mortars on Corporal Sahs and his men who were wrestling with the assault boat on the beach. Sahs was hit in the wrist and a soldier named Manuel Gonzalez was shot in the back as he jumped from the boat. The rest of the assault boat detail made it to the cover of the jungle uninjured. Sahs crawled out to the severely injured Gonzalez and dragged him to safety behind a log. Japanese mortar shells began falling on Benson's position and one other member of Company G was wounded before the Japanese mortar was knocked out by the mortars of the company's weapons platoon.[10] Bruce relished any opportunity to use the 60mm mortar that he slogged pieces of and ammunition for through the jungle. He and the rest of Company G's weapons platoon had become deadly with the weapon.[11]

The following day, February 3, Benson planned an all-out assault on the Japanese position. Heavy mortars from 2nd Battalion's Company M and their crews were brought up to give Benson's men more firepower. Under a steady rain of fire from the 81mm mortars of Company M and the company's own 60mm mortars as well as fire from the company's light machine gun, 1st and 2nd Platoon were able to cross the river in the Japanese assault boat under a smattering of enemy fire.

Under the command of Sergeant Horace Gamas, 1st Platoon crossed the sixty yards of sand and plunged into the jungle where they found several well-hidden Japanese dugouts, but no enemy soldiers. The rest of Benson's men crossed the river in the assault boat without incident. Once reunited the GIs pushed forward another 400 yards where they discovered another Japanese camp and began a search. As the men of Gamas's 1st Platoon fanned out through the camp two Japanese machine guns opened fire, killing one American, mortally wounding another, and wounding four more members of Company G less seriously.[12] One GI had a bullet pierce the front of his helmet, but miraculously the bullet did not penetrate his head and instead creased the soldier's scalp.[13] Sergeant Gamas crawled back to the rest of the company and mortar fire was directed at the locations of the enemy machine guns. Benson, at the head of 3rd Platoon, resumed the American assault but was also thrown back. The company dug in and established a perimeter a few hundred yards from the Japanese position and spent an anxious night waiting for a counterattack that never came.

Bruce Baird was among the less seriously wounded men on February 3. His squad crossed the river during the early stages of the assault and he and another man acted as scouts exploring a trail leading away from the original Japanese position. At a division in the trail Baird and the other man separated, with the other man going left and Baird right. A machine gun opened fire on the other man and Baird returned to the rest of his squad to tell them what had happened and where he thought the Japanese were before heading back down the trail to see about the other scout. When he got close to the place where he and the other man had separated there was a burst of machine-gun fire and one of the bullets pierced his leg just above the knee, but it did not hit bone. Down and unable to walk Baird squirmed over the trunk of a downed palm tree which gave him cover. A single Japanese rifle shot indicated to Baird that in all likelihood the other man had been killed. Separated from his rifle and certain that Japanese soldiers would locate his position any minute, Baird managed to crawl fifty yards back up the trail towards his squad before a medic taking cover on the trail got his attention and signaled for him to crawl over to where he was. The medic supported Baird as they hopped back to the rest of Company G. There medics loaded him on a raft and floated him back across the river where he joined the other wounded men—one of whom died during the night. The next morning, Baird and the other wounded men were loaded on a boat and evacuated to Sanananda Point. From there Baird was transferred to a hospital facility at Oro Bay. He missed the rest of the Kumusi River patrol. It would be months before he rejoined Company G.[14]

Benson renewed Company G's attack on February 4 but was again driven back by machine-gun fire directed at his men with eerie accuracy. Regimental Commander Colonel Jens A. Doe came looking for Benson's command in a Higgins boat and Benson traveled back to Sebari village to meet him. Company G had been out of contact with regimental command for more than a day due to a broken radio and Doe had literally come forward to find Benson's lost command. He found Company G low on supplies, with several wounded in need of evacuation, and several men too sick with malaria to continue.[15] Benson's manpower was so reduced after only four days that the company merged its three rifle platoons into just two. The conditions under which the men were moving, hiking, and fighting were so severe that Doe sent a platoon from Company L of the 163rd forward to reinforce the patrol.[16] The lack of supplies and water occasionally drove Bruce to extremes. During one of the fights, along one of the rivers they crossed, he remembered being so thirsty that he risked his life to lean out beyond an eddy where blood had pooled to fill his canteen. Saturated with river water, sweat, and mud, his uniform began to decay while he wore it. He and the other men ran through their rations quickly, but because the company was occasionally out of touch with Battalion Command, resupply was spotty, and Bruce frequently went hungry.[17]

Sometime late on February 4 or early on February 5, Company G captured a Japanese tree platform hidden high and deep in the jungle. It was this position that had allowed the Japanese to see Company G's movements and direct such accurate fire on the Americans. With this position taken, Benson put in motion a plan to catch the remaining Japanese in a trap. He sent the platoon from Company L and the platoon from the 186th's Company G to flank the Japanese position by moving through the jungle to cut off their escape route while Company G resumed their assault on the Japanese position. Rather than driving the Japanese into a trap, his maneuver drove the Japanese into the positions of the unprepared men of the flanking platoons that had not been able to get into position in time. As a result, most of the Japanese Kombela garrison escaped.[18]

During the Kumusi patrol Anderson became the acting commander of his platoon when Lieutenant Braman was temporarily knocked out of action. During a rest period, Captain Benson asked Anderson to provide the name of a man who would act as his messenger. Anderson replied that he could not spare a man to act as the captain's servant and Benson busted him down to the rank of private and sent him back to his platoon. Though officially he was only a private and a company scout, because the men respected him and the sergeant named to act as platoon commander did not really want the job, Anderson retained command of his platoon. He was soon returned to the rank of sergeant.[19]

February 6 began with a few hours of trudging through heavy jungle to the mouth of the Bukumbari River where all the elements of Benson's command were reunited. On the 7th, the GIs continued toward their objective with the platoon from the 186th in the lead. That afternoon the Americans reached an unnamed river and observed a Japanese position on the other side. A Higgins boat had been brought up, probably to bring supplies to Benson's patrol, and the men of the 186th attempted to use it to launch an amphibious assault on the beach near the Japanese encampment. During the attack, the boat's coxswain turned back under heavy machine-gun fire. The next morning, with the heavy mortars from Company M, the mortars of Company G's weapons platoon and an Australian 25-pound artillery piece, the platoon from the 186th repeated the previous day's attack and this time landed successfully. They pushed into the Japanese position while the men of Company G crossed the river in two salvaged Japanese assault boats. The two combat groups converged on an abandoned Japanese hospital where they discovered the bodies of several recently deceased enemy soldiers but found no live Japanese soldiers. The morning of the 9th kicked off with a long hike through dense jungle and across several unnamed rivers with little enemy contact. The biggest event of that day was a swim across a wide inlet during which the men floated their equipment on improvised rafts. By nightfall they were within six miles of the Kumusi River. They covered those six miles on February 10. At the Kumusi River, Benson's men dug in and began securing their position and conducting mop-up patrols in the area with limited but regular contact with elements of the Japanese army.[20] Their river front perimeter gave the men of Company G a chance to bathe regularly for the first time in weeks. Bruce and the other men took full advantage until their indigenous guides told them the river was home to man-eating crocodiles. After that the men only went into the water up to their knees.[21]

Jack Anderson who seemed to have a knack for fun and mischief found an opportunity to take the men of Company G's minds off their misery for an evening. After the company reached the Kumusi River, supplies of food reached them with greater regularity. In one of the loads of airdropped supplies, Company G received several pounds of flour. At first they did not know what to do with the flour, but when the men found baking powder among the supplies left behind by the Japanese, Anderson and another man decided to make pancakes. They used whatever metal materials they could find for griddles and started to mix up the pancake batter only to find that the flour was full of weevils. With a group of hungry men who they had promised a pancake supper to keep happy, Anderson and the other man decided to make the pancakes anyway figuring what the men did not know would not hurt them and that the weevils would just add a little meat to their diets. They joined in, eating as many of the weevil-speckled pancakes as anyone and no one caught on or complained.[22]

On Valentine's Day 1943, Benson's men were relieved by the men of the 163rd's Company L. Company G boarded landing craft which quickly carried them back to Killerton and Sanananda Point. From there they would get four or five months' worth of time to recuperate at Popondetta village near the airstrip where they and the rest of the 163rd had arrived in New Guinea in early January.

The importance of the Kumusi River patrol to U.S. plans in New Guinea is indicated by the resources and reinforcements that battalion and division leadership committed to its success. The mission was a qualified success. Company G, and attached units, covered twenty-two miles in ten days through dense mosquito-infested jungle, crossed rivers named and unnamed, and faced tough opposition. They reduced several Japanese positions and cut off a means of escape for the Japanese soldiers still trapped in the jungle interior of New Guinea. However, despite Captain Benson's skillful handling of his men and resources, it is likely that several hundred Japanese soldiers escaped to fight at a different location. It is unlikely that any of the remaining members of Company G cared much about the mission's success. They had reached their objective and survived. The cost to the Company was high. When Company G took up its first combat position on January 9 it was near its full complement of around 170 men. When the company left on the Kumusi River patrol there were only eighty-eight members of the company fit for service. Only forty of those men made the boat trip back to Killerton on Valentine's Day 1943. During the patrol, Japanese rifles, machine guns, and mortars had claimed the lives of three members of the company and an additional ten were wounded. But malaria took out thirty-five members of the company who were so sick they had to be evacuated. In all, in just over one month of fighting, Company G's strength had been reduced by almost three fourths.[23] A picture of the survivors of the Kumusi patrol shows an emaciated, ragged, and haggard group of men. Bruce, Anderson, and the others had earned their rest.[24]

CHAPTER 5

Rest for Some, Combat for Others

February 15, 1943–July 14, 1943

By the time the men of Company G boarded transport boats to take them from their Kumusi River base back to the Buna–Sanananda area for a period of rest away from the front lines, the area that just weeks before they had fought and died for under the worst of conditions was being transformed. Army engineers with the help of the "Angels" had constructed more permanent hospital and supply facilities and had even built roads connecting key locations to one another. This gave Company G the opportunity to take their first ride in trucks during the war.[1]

During the Sanananda campaign two of the 41st Division's three regimental combat teams had seen action. The 163rd Regiment, the first of the division's regiments to fight, had been used extensively and suffered significant casualties due to enemy action and disease. The 186th Regiment which arrived second and played an important role in the last stages of the campaign had also suffered in the heat, humidity, and mosquito infested swamps of Papua New Guinea. These two regiments remained in the Buna–Sanananda–Gona region after the end of major combat operations in February of 1943. Only the 162nd Regiment had yet to see action having spent the first two months of 1943 in the safety of the division's camps in Australia. That would change beginning in spring and carrying through to the summer of 1943.[2]

Though it probably seemed longer to the men of the 163rd and 186th, they had only been in New Guinea for two months when elements of the 162nd and other parts of the division began arriving. The division's battalion of engineers arrived and went to work building roads, airfields, and fortifications to turn the Buna–Gona area into a base of operation for the next phase of the fight for Papua New Guinea. As the battalions from the 162nd filtered into New Guinea via the sea and overland marches, they began to replace companies from the 163rd and 186th in the defensive positions they held at Sanananda.

Despite the relaxed atmosphere in the reserve areas, the division was preparing for the next phase of the army's New Guinea campaign. This time the 162nd Regiment would play a role in General MacArthur's plan to reduce and capture the large Japanese base at Rabaul on the nearby Island of New Britain.[3]

As a part of MacArthur's plan named Operation *Cartwheel*, the main target of which was Rabaul, the 162nd acting as an adjunct force in concert with the Australian 3rd and 5th Divisions would take part in driving the Japanese from the Salamaua region of New Guinea which lay north along the island's coast from the Buna–Gona region.

The Salamaua campaign was a difficult assignment. The 162nd fought against a large enemy force in harsh terrain for months. The dense jungle, hills, and ridges made planning combat operations on a large scale difficult, and most planning was confined to maneuvering troops only at the platoon level. One of the lessons Allied command had learned in the fighting in the Buna–Sanananda–Gona region was how to effectively utilize mortars and artillery to reduce enemy positions before assaulting them directly. This kept casualties lower. Some of the toughest fighting of the campaign involved clearing the Japanese from the ridges overlooking the strategically important Nassau Bay. That mission fell to the 162nd's 2nd Battalion which was under the command of Archie Roosevelt, the son of former President Teddy Roosevelt. Archie Roosevelt was a decorated veteran of World War I, but when World War II began, he petitioned the army and Franklin Roosevelt for a combat command position. He was made a major and put in charge of the 2nd Battalion. Under his leadership, 2nd Battalion captured the ridge which was renamed Roosevelt Ridge in his honor.

The 162nd's fight for Salamaua lasted from June 1943 till the beginning of September of 1943. Because of the 162nd's contribution to Operation *Cartwheel* the Japanese lost Rabaul. The regiment paid a high price for the part they played in the victory. Eighty-nine men of the regiment died in combat during those three months, but at the end of the Salamaua campaign the U.S. Army had wrested control of Eastern New Guinea from the Japanese and set the stage for more offensive actions moving forward.[4]

While the 162nd Regiment began their fight for Salamaua, the 163rd Regiment moved into division reserve and, for a time, their combat in New Guinea came to an end. The regiment received a Special Unit Citation from President Roosevelt for the role they played in clearing the Japanese from the Killerton Track and securing Sanananda Point. The citation allowed the men of the regiment to wear a special ribbon on the pocket of their dress uniforms. But even in the reserve areas in New Guinea, the men of the 163rd would have few, if any, opportunities to don their dress uniforms.

By the time division command placed the 163rd in reserve, the regiment had lost ninety-seven men in combat, an additional 215 had been wounded, and most of the men had been sickened by malaria, scrub typhus, dysentery, or dengue fever. Of those diseases, malaria proved the most difficult to treat and the regiment discovered that the best solution was to prevent soldiers from contracting it with drugs and mosquito eradication. Though this was more of a benefit to the replacements who would join the regiment than the veterans of the fighting around Sanananda.[5]

The regiment's companies assigned to rear areas were still expected to conduct patrols around their camps. These patrols guarded against snipers and dealt with Japanese stragglers who had been abandoned when the main Japanese forces retreated. From time to time those patrols found evidence of one or two Japanese soldiers hiding in the jungle nearby, but few of them were interested in fighting anymore.[6] Most just tried to survive by sneaking into the American camps and stealing food and anything else they could get their hands on. Still, the GIs found far more dead Japanese soldiers than live ones and were often given the unpleasant task of burying the putrefying bodies in the jungle. They made no effort to identify the Japanese dead or to record the places they were buried.[7] More frightening and damaging than the random encounters with enemy soldiers were the Japanese air raids. Still, the men in reserve had time on their hands. Though entertainment options were limited, the men found ways to amuse themselves.[8]

Their more fixed locations and their reduced responsibilities gave the men of the 163rd the chance to get to know the indigenous people of New Guinea better. The people the Americans dubbed "Angels" continued to act as nurses and hospital staff in the rear areas occupied by the 163rd. The large number of GIs sickened by tropical disease crowded hospitals at division headquarters, forcing even very ill men to remain in makeshift medical facilities at the battalion level where there were not enough trained medical staff to care for all of them. For many GIs, their primary caregivers during their illness were indigenous men. These devotion of these "Angels" earned the love and respect of the Americans. In addition to working in hospitals, the "Angels" also helped the American military by clearing land and constructing camp facilities.[9] Proximity gave American soldiers a chance to observe aspects of the "Angels'" daily lives. On Sundays the "Angels" gathered for communal dances which the Americans sometimes participated in. GIs who smoked learned to tolerate the incredibly strong tobacco the "Angels" smoked. And a few even tried chewing betel nuts—the narcotic effect of which most of the "Angels" seemed to be addicted to. Few Americans could tolerate the bitter material for long and they did not like the way it stained their teeth red.[10]

One thing that could not be helped was the heat and the humidity of the New Guinea climate. The end of major combat operations in the area around Sanananda in February brought some relief in the form of an improved supply situation. Food and replacement clothes as well as equipment arrived in greater quantities and improved in quality. For entertainment, traveling theater troops came to perform for the men. One group put on a show that involved singing and dancing. Since the troop had no female cast members, male actors dressed as women and played the female parts. They were so convincing that many of the men of the 163rd did not believe that they were men.

During the regiment's time in reserve, female nurses began arriving to staff the field hospitals behind the front lines. A date with one of these nurses was a special event for the few men lucky enough to get one, though the necessity of the soldier carrying their M1 with them probably put a limit on romance. The precaution of moving around camp armed remained necessary because of the few Japanese soldiers hiding out in the 163rd's reserve area. Violent encounters were rare but there were a few incidents. The most common interaction with the Japanese military for the men of the 163rd were air raids. Japanese bombers and dive-bombers became a common sight, but the improved accuracy of American and Australian anti-aircraft gunners minimized the danger.[11]

When Company G was relieved from their position near Sanananda, regimental command ordered them inland to protect an emergency airstrip near Popondetta village. The Japanese had built the airstrip during their invasion and occupation of the island, but the Allies had captured it in the early days of the fight for Buna–Sanananda–Gona. The company rode in trucks over a newly created road that connected Sanananda to Popondetta. Their new location seemed like a bit of paradise to the sick and weary survivors of the Kumusi River patrol.[12]

Jack Anderson of Company G described the location as just such a paradise. Located high enough above the coastal plain that mosquitoes were not as much of a problem, the higher location also offered the men some relief from the heat and humidity of the jungle.

The men of Company G welcomed the relocation to their new home and their new assignment. They lived in eight-men tents (pup tents had not yet been issued) and discovered that the best way to ventilate the tents involved raising the center pole a foot or two higher than designed and then cutting shorter poles from the surrounding trees and placing them so they held the sides of the tent out parallel to the ground creating a wider canopy with open sides. This meant they could maximize the cool breezes, but it also meant that snakes and other critters could walk or slither through their shelters. To avoid waking up eye-to-eye with a snake or other animal, and to keep dry, the men built hammock-like sleeping platforms out of tree branches cut from the jungle around them. Even this precaution did not completely eliminate the problem as one machine gunner from Company H stationed with Company G found out. He woke up with a huge python in his cot and when he jumped up and ran out of his tent, he fell down a bluff and broke his leg. Animals were not the only danger in the jungle. Anderson found out that even the trees could cause pain. He and one of his tent-mates made the mistake of cutting several branches to make tent flap poles from a tree with poisonous sap and spent several days covered in raised welts and with their eyes swollen shut.

There remained some danger of enemy activity in the area. The regular Company G patrols through the jungle around the airstrip resulted in encounters with a few Japanese soldiers. The reality was that their patrols were scavenging expeditions during which they searched for abandoned Japanese equipment and food. The jungle did provide them with a steady supply of bananas, papayas, and coconuts which the men used to supplement their rations.

Boredom became as big an issue as anything. With time on their hands, the men learned new skills to pass the time. Some made jewelry

Soldiers of the 41st Division examine the wreckage of a Japanese "Zero" destroyed in the bombing of a Japanese airstrip in the Buna area in 1942. (National Archives)

by bending and shaping Australian coins into rings and they even figured out how to inlay the rings with color by melting plastic.

During this period of inactivity, friends Jack Anderson and Doyle Bruce took it upon themselves to teach one of their friends, a private named William Mayberry, how to read and write. Like Bruce, Mayberry was from Texas, but he had not attended school regularly enough to have learned prior to joining the army. That did not stop Mayberry's family from writing to him nor did that stop him from wanting to write them back, which meant Bruce and Anderson spent time reading Mayberry's letters to him and writing his letters home for him. The solution for Bruce and Anderson was to teach Mayberry to read. They started by teaching him the alphabet and the sounds the letters made. He soon learned to write and read simple words, and within a month, he could read and write his own letters home. Mayberry's handwriting was so bad that the censors who opened and read all mail the soldiers wrote home did not send any of Mayberry's letters back. Bruce and Anderson spent several weeks working to improve his handwriting. When the censors sent back one of Mayberry's letters, they figured their work was done and the lessons ended.

On July 15, 1943, Company G and the rest of the 163rd Regiment began the trip to an even better rest location—Australia. Company G flew back over the Owen Stanley Mountains that they had first crossed in January and landed at Port Moresby where they stayed until troopships arrived to transport them back to Gladstone.[13]

CHAPTER 6

Return to Australia

July 14, 1943–March 23, 1944

The 41st Division returned to Australia from New Guinea in the same order in which they had left at the end of 1942 and the beginning of 1943. The 163rd Regiment began its trip back to Rockhampton during the second week of July 1943 and arrived a few weeks later. The 186th left a few weeks after them and the 162nd, which had completed a long stint in combat securing Salamaua and Nassau Bay on the New Guinea Coast, embarked for Australia on September 25. By late October almost all of the 41st Division's units, save a battalion of the 162nd and some support groups, were back in their old camp at Rockhampton.[1]

The first stop on the 163rds journey back to Australia was Port Moresby, New Guinea, where the men received six months' worth of mail all at once. The packages, letters, newspapers, and magazines—which they had assumed were lost—were now theirs to read and enjoy, though packing that much mail along with their gear on board the Dutch merchantman that acted as a troopship must have presented some challenges. This ship was more comfortable than the ship that had brought them to New Guinea in January and the food was better. When the regiment disembarked at Gladstone they were met by the people of that small town who welcomed their new heroes. The men did not get to enjoy their hero's welcome for long. Unusually, the troop trains that would take them to their old camp at Rockhampton were waiting for them when they arrived.[2]

When the troopships that carried the 163rd back to Australia docked at Gladstone, Dorothy Henderson, June Connellan, and her parents were there to greet Jack Anderson and Doyle Bruce. They would not get to spend much time together at that time, but the 163rd's long stay in Australia gave them a chance to resume their relationships.[3]

Bruce Baird took a different route back to Australia and the 163rd. While the other men of Company G finished the Kumusi patrol and took up residence near Popondetta in the hills of Papua New Guinea, Baird received treatment for his wounded leg at an army hospital at Oro Bay. During his first week there his malaria returned, and he was sick for more than a week. The hospital staff could offer little relief beyond cool rags to reduce his feverishness. In time his symptoms dissipated, and he felt well again. The staff decided he was too sick to return to Company G, but not sick or hurt enough to be sent back to the United States, so they sent him to another army medical facility near Brisbane, Australia. There Baird, when healthy, worked as an orderly assisting the hospital staff by collecting samples from patients. He enjoyed the proximity to the entertainment available in town and in Brisbane. In June he was ordered to go to the army's replacement center located at a horse track in Brisbane. The staff there informed him that he had been reclassified as medical personnel and would not be rejoining his infantry unit. He appreciated the doctors that recommended him for reclassification, but he wanted to rejoin Company G. Another relapse of malaria put him back in the hospital where he was given quinine, which made him ill. When well again he set out for Rockhampton to rejoin his company, arriving in early August.[4]

Back in Rockhampton the 163rd easily settled into their old camp area because much of the camp they had built in 1942 remained. Since they were the first regiment from the 41st to arrive, they did little, and their officers seemed in no hurry to begin the next round of training.[5] Many of the details of military discipline were ignored during those weeks. Few, if any, soldiers wore any indications of their rank, a leftover from standard combat practices, and the men could do whatever they wanted during the evenings. The only requirement was to report for morning roll call.[6]

The relaxed atmosphere in camp and the free time available during the early days of their second stay in Australia gave the men of Company G time to notice and interact with some of the wildlife in the

Rockhampton area. Anderson's squad noticed a huge snake draped among the high branches of a tree near the edge of the area where they were camped and decided to get the snake down so they could see it. Since none of them had any interest in climbing high in the tree to wrestle the snake down they decided to shake the slender tree instead in the hopes that the snake would climb or fall down. They took turns shaking the tree for hours and eventually the snake lost its grip and fell. The men of Anderson's group looked at the snake for a while but for the most part left it alone. After some time, the snake crawled back up into the tree and Anderson's squad adopted it as a mascot. Men from other squads came by to look at the snake until one night it slithered down the tree and disappeared. There were also goanna, giant screaming lizards, startled many of the men who walked to near them, but they were mostly harmless.[7]

There were two new things for the men during their second stay in Australia: seven-day R&R passes that included travel time allowances and a special hospital for men who had contracted malaria or other tropical diseases. The seven-day passes were most welcome and many of the men used them to travel extensively within Australia. One group of men even made it all the way down to Tasmania during their leave. A stay at the malaria hospital, which, mysteriously was named "The Fox Farm," was not as welcome, but it wasn't that bad either. Technically the hospital called "The Fox Farm" was Company L of the 6th Army Training Center. There the medical staff took good care of the men and made sure they were comfortable. But they also experimented on their patients with an anti-malarial drug called Atabrine. The experiments mainly involved giving higher doses of the drug to see if it could cure malaria as well as prevent it. The higher doses made some men sick and caused the skin of some men to turn yellow. Atabrine proved to be a good preventative for malaria, but for men who had already contracted the disease it offered little relief from their recurring symptoms. For relief, the men swore by quinine and aspirin.[8]

The men quickly adjusted to the routine of life in camp and enjoyed some well-earned rest. That period of relaxation did not last because training for the division's next mission had to begin. Over the course of their second stay in Australia, all three of the division's infantry regiments spent time at Toorbul Point practicing amphibious landings using new landing craft and under the supervision of the U.S. Navy. While the 41st recovered in Australia the War in the Pacific shifted into high gear. Based on their training the men speculated that their next mission would be a big one. Meanwhile the army's new rotation system went into effect and men who had earned enough points along with the sick and wounded from the fight in New Guinea began to rotate back to the United States. This meant the division had to bring in new recruits, assign them to their units, and train them.[9] Most of the replacement soldiers were younger than those from the first round of the draft like Baird and Doyle Bruce. According to Baird the replacement troops spent too much time thinking about earning points for rotation back to the United States. For he and the other veterans of Sanananda, home seemed too far away to worry about counting rotation points. Owing to their service in New Guinea and the depleted nature of Company G's ranks many veterans received promotions. Both Bruce Baird and Doyle Bruce were promoted to Sergeant during their second stay in Australia.[10]

Though the men complained about the repetitive nature of their training and the physical effort required, the U.S. Army's dependence on small-unit actions and tactics meant that every soldier had to know his job inside and out. The ability of small units and individual soldiers to adjust automatically to changing situations in order to carry out combat missions with minimal direction provided the foundation for the success of the regiment. This was the 163rd's last real opportunity to receive training and what they learned would have to last them through the remainder of the war.[11] As training intensified so did military discipline. Bruce Baird got in trouble with the army censors for sending a photo home. He had asked his family to make copies and send them back so that he

Doyle Edward Bruce, taken sometime after Company G's return to Australia in 1943, with 41st Division shoulder patch and sergeant stripes visible. (Collection of Sharon Bruce)

could share them with some of the other men. When those men started to send their copies of the picture home the censor noticed that there was a beer keg visible in the picture with the name of the brewery on it and identified the picture as a security risk that could give away the location of Baird's unit to the enemy. To clear himself, Baird had to ask his family to return his original photo that had been stamped approved by an earlier army censor.[12]

The camp at Rockhampton had undergone some improvements since Company G's first stay there. The tents the men slept in had been upgraded with places to store equipment. A PX (post exchange) opened to provide snacks and other small comfort items. A kitchen with a wooden floor had been constructed and because it was one of the places on base with electricity the men who were off-duty could go there to read or write letters home. The kitchen also hosted dances to which young women from Rockhampton came, with chaperones. There was a bus that the men could take into Rockhampton to see a movie or shop that ran about every half hour. In September, Eleanor Roosevelt made a quick tour by car of the American base at Rockhampton though not many of the men were aware of it while it was happening.[13]

Good friends Jack Anderson and Doyle Bruce not only had the shared experiences of combat as a part of the same unit, they also had Australian "girlfriends" who were good friends with each other and lived in Gladstone. Bruce and June Connellan had become close during Company G's brief assignment to guard the port at Gladstone itself in 1942 and Bruce and June had introduced Anderson to Dorothy Henderson. There is no evidence that these relationships were anything but chaste, but the attraction presented by June and Dorothy was strong enough that Bruce and Anderson spent most of their time on leave in Gladstone.

Most often Bruce and Anderson made the seventy-mile trip from Rockhampton to Gladstone by train which took a slow, roundabout route between the two towns. At some point Anderson made friends with a Rockhampton cab driver who lived in Gladstone and who would drive Anderson and Bruce there when he could get enough gas to make the trip. Rationing in Australia limited civilian supplies of gas, eggs, flour, and clothing among other things. For accommodation they stayed nights at Mrs. Henderson's public house. Australian law said that for a pub to have a bar it also had to act as a rooming house.

Anderson made friends with Mrs. Henderson who was also fond of Bruce so all they had to do was phone before they left for Gladstone, and she would have a room for them.[14]

Gladstone did not offer many entertainment options, so Anderson and Bruce spent time at the pub, on the beach with June and Dorothy, or, more often, at the Connellans' home. The Connellans treated both men like family members and Bruce and Anderson called Mrs. Connellan "Ma Connellan." She baked for them and made meals for them, and in return they brought her food items from the army base and worked around the house to help the Connellans out. Part of the attraction of Gladstone was almost certainly the possibility for romance with June and Dorothy, but the Connellan house and family served as a source of comfort for two young men far from home.[15]

For their part, the Connellans felt true affection for Bruce and Anderson and maintained a correspondence with both men and their families for the duration of the war. A letter written by Ma Connellan to Anderson's mother on March 3, 1944, makes it clear that she and Anderson's mother had already written to one another. In the letter "Ma Connellan" praised Anderson's kindness and listed all the eggs and kitchen items that he had gotten for the family. She closed the letter by assuring Anderson's mother that she and her husband would do everything they could to make him comfortable while he was in Australia.[16]

December 25, 1943, saw the men of the 41st celebrate their second Christmas away from home. Australian Christmas traditions were different than American customs. There were no colored lights or Douglas Fir Christmas trees. There were presents and packages from home which the men opened as soon as they got them, believing they would be deployed any day and would not be able to take their presents with them or enjoy them if they waited till Christmas Day. As it turned out they could have waited to open their presents. It would be another three months before the 163rd left Australia again.[17]

Anderson had a better Christmas than most of his comrades. He got a seven-day pass that covered Christmas and used it to join the Connellans at their vacation home on Boyne Island. That Dorothy Henderson would be spending the holiday at her family's vacation home nearby was likely the main source of attraction. He and Dorothy spent most of that time loafing on the beach. Anderson thought it funny that the otherwise reserved and proper Dorothy and her friends felt no embarrassment changing into their swimsuits on the beach hidden only by a towel held up by a friend. He asked Dorothy if they were ever alone at the beach if she would do so while he held the towel and closed his eyes. Her answer made it clear that there were limits to how familiar she was willing to become with him. Yet she clearly had strong feelings for him. When she unexpectedly found him in the kitchen of her family's place one morning before breakfast drinking shots of whisky from a teaspoon, she became very angry, went up to her room to put on her swimsuit (which was a gift from Anderson), and then came down and dragged Anderson to the beach. There she essentially called him a fool and gave him a lecture on the fact that her uncles were just trying to get him drunk.[18]

Near the end of the 163rd's second stay in Australia, Doyle Bruce received orders to go to Brisbane to do guard duty. It was a three-month assignment that he remembered fondly. There were Saturday horse races, plenty of beer, a vibrant nightlife, and a wealth of pretty women in the city.[19] Bruce must have continued to write the Connellans throughout the war because when they learned that he had finally earned enough points to rotate home in June of 1945, they wrote to congratulate him for getting to go home as well as for earning a Purple Heart. Most of the letter caught Bruce up on the doings of the family. Ma Connellan rather pointedly informed him that June had gotten a job in Brisbane and was seeing a bank manager. The letter also expressed the Connellans' affection for Bruce and their gratitude for what he and the other Americans had done for Australia. She expressed pride in the fact that she and her husband had provided a homelike refuge for him and had taken care of him for his parents while he was so far away from home. She closed her letter with a wistful reminder of how Bruce had helped the family cut back the hedge and expressed a hope that if he had the chance he would come and help them with it again.[20]

Doyle Bruce would not return to Australia during the war. The time he spent with the Connellans in 1943 was his last experience of any place like home until the war ended.

CHAPTER 7

Hollandia and Aitape

March 23, 1944–May 17, 1944

During the 41st Division's second stint in Australia new recruits and draftees began arriving to fill out the ranks of the companies that had lost men to combat and disease during the fighting in New Guinea. One of those new men was Private Hargis Westerfield from Indiana. Westerfield had been a member of an Ohio National Guard cavalry unit before the war and had a college education. At thirty-four years of age Westerfield was older than most men in the army and certainly one of the oldest men assigned to Company G of the 163rd Infantry. His age did not make up for the disparity in experience between himself and his younger comrades who had been through the fighting in New Guinea in 1943. Aitape would be his first time in combat and he had a lot to learn about jungle warfare and his Japanese enemies.[1]

While the 41st Division rested and trained in Australia, the fight for New Guinea continued. The Australian Army took Lae across the Gulf of Huon from Salamaua, where the 162nd Regiment had successfully battled the Japanese in September, and Finschhafen further north along the New Guinea coast. The 41st's next objective lay 400 miles to the northwest of Finschhafen, but until March of 1944, neither they nor the Japanese knew that.

In early March of 1944 advanced elements of the division began leaving Australia for a return to New Guinea. MacArthur's new offensive had already begun. The army's First Cavalry Division fought the Japanese for control of New Britain and the Admiralty Islands that lay to the north of New Guinea and the 24th Infantry Division moved into the new Allied

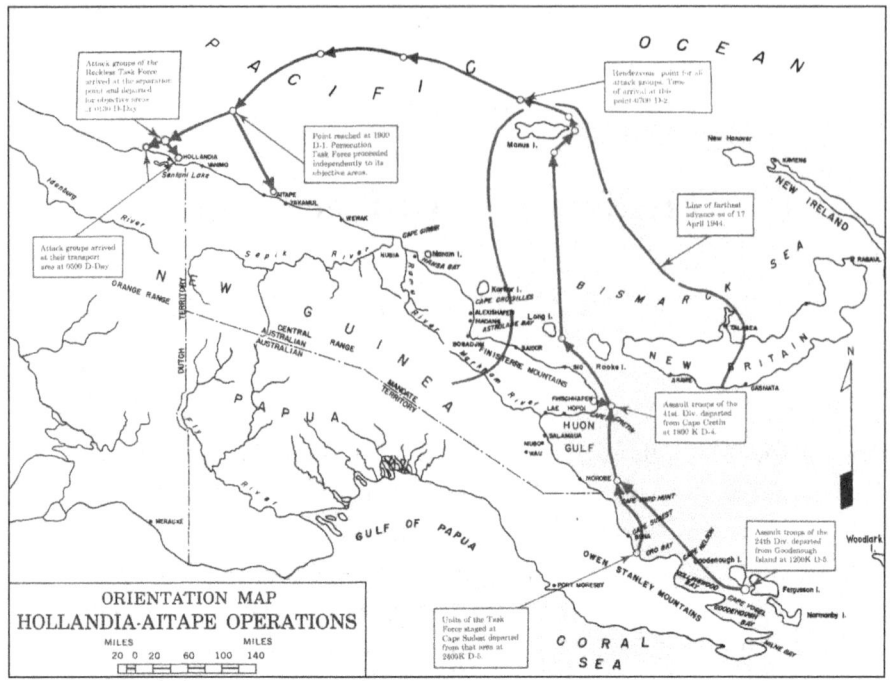

Map showing the movement of the 41st Division to Hollandia and Aitape in March of 1944. (U.S. Army Center of Military History)

staging area at Finschhafen. By the middle of the month, most of the 41st had boarded ships at Gladstone Harbor and began their journey to Finschhafen. The bulk of the division arrived by March 23 and found an impressive military base and a harbor filled with ships and landing craft waiting for them. Army engineer bulldozers were busily building roads, finishing construction on the new 6th Army headquarters, and a semi-permanent camp big enough to house an entire division. The 41st would remain at Finschhafen for a week before boarding transport ships for their next combat mission.[2]

For Jack Anderson the relocation to Finschhafen revealed just how much progress the U.S. military had made while he and the other men of the 41st were in Australia. Instead of sailing from Gladstone to Finschhafen on Dutch cargo ships that were never made to transport thousands of men from one place to another, brand new American built troopships called "Liberty Ships" carried them to their new base.

When they arrived the number of big ships in the newly constructed harbor at Finschhafen impressed Anderson. He and the other men of Company G enjoyed getting to stay in a camp they did not have to build, use latrines they did not have to dig, eat hot food, receive mail, and have no training or patrols to carry out for an entire week.[3] The army did issue them two new pieces of equipment, bazookas which they found to be mostly useless, and grenade launchers which they did find useful.[4]

Under General MacArthur's leadership the U.S. and Australian Armies had made a series of short jumps along the coast of New Guinea—Buna to Salamaua, Salamaua to Lae, Lae to Finschhafen—while simultaneously clearing the Admiralty Islands of enemy forces. The next jump would be a much longer and more ambitious move that bypassed a major Japanese military base at Wewak and instead landed three divisions on the other side of that Japanese stronghold. Allied planes kept the Japanese base at Wewak under a steady bombardment in an effort to convince the Japanese commander that an attack on the base would happen soon. The American ruse was so effective that the Japanese commander moved part of the garrison at Hollandia to Wewak to reinforce his base. Ironically, Hollandia was the target of MacArthur's next attack. He believed that if the U.S. Army could take Hollandia they could isolate and neutralize the large Japanese force at Wewak and gain complete control of New Guinea. The plan involved secretly moving the 41st, 32nd and 24th Divisions from Finschhafen to the New Guinea coastline around Hollandia. When the Americans boarded their transport ships, they joined a huge armada headed north from Finschhafen towards the Admiralty Islands in a further effort to deceive the Japanese about the location of the Allied attack. This move would also keep the American armada out of the range of Japanese scout planes before it began its sweeping move to the southwest. The deception worked perfectly, and when they landed the GIs would face lighter resistance than even MacArthur expected.

For the attack on Hollandia the 41st Division was divided into two separate task forces. The 186th and the 162nd Regiments, along with three of the division's Field Artillery Battalions, and the 24th Division made up the Reckless Task Force that would launch a two-pronged attack at Hollandia. The 163rd Regiment, along with elements of the 32nd Division, and one of the 41st Division's Field Artillery Battalions made up the Persecution Task Force that would land to the east of Aitape. Just off the coast of New Guinea, the huge armada of troopships, carriers, battleships, and other surface ships split up, with a third of the ships and men headed to Aitape and the other two-thirds for Hollandia.

Both attacks involved thousands of infantry men and the men of support units, dozens of ships, hundreds of amphibious landing craft, and planes launched from carriers or taking off from the new airfields at Finschhafen. To pull off the attack MacArthur had to coordinate the efforts of the U.S. Army, the Australian military, and the U.S. Navy. Given the complexity of the plan, it went remarkably well.[5]

The Reckless Task Force hit the beaches around the settlement of Hollandia in three places. The 24th Division landed farther west along the coast from Hollandia, while the 162nd and 186th Divisions hit the beaches south of Hollandia along Humbolt Bay and moved inland.

The 3rd Battalion of the 162nd landed on the beach near Hollandia and met no resistance. Thanks to Japanese command's decision to move most of the Hollandia garrison to Wewak, most of the Japanese soldiers were not combat troops and they fled to the hills during the naval bombardment that preceded the landing. The 3rd Battalion was followed onto the beach by the 1st and 2nd Battalions, as well as tanks, engineers, and field artillery, as the 3rd pushed north into the hills and prepared to take Hollandia town. The 162nd's first day of fighting came to an end with only one significant event. A Japanese bomber caused a serious incident when one of the bombs it dropped on the American-held beach hit an abandoned Japanese ammo dump which then ignited an Allied fuel depot. A huge fire erupted injuring several American GIs and endangering some artillery pieces nearby. The fireball and column of smoke were visible from a great distance. Within a few days of landing, the 162nd had taken Hollandia town and moved north along the coast of Humbolt Bay, destroying elements of the Japanese army where they found them and rendezvousing with elements of the 24th Division to take a Japanese airfield.

After landing at Hollandia, the 186th Regiment moved inland from the beaches to capture two airdromes which were their main objectives. With the exception of an accidental strafing by an American fighter plane that mistook the men of the 186th for the Japanese, the landing was without incident. Having secured the first two airdromes, the regiment continued pushing towards a third. The Japanese had managed to gather around 400 men in the hills near the drome. Companies B and C of the 1st Battalion attacked the Japanese positions on April 27 but were repulsed. On April 29 the entire Battalion, following a barrage from the field artillery, attacked and overran the Japanese position killing scores of the enemy.

Military planners felt the operation had gone nearly perfectly but knew that part of the success on the ground was due to the shortsightedness of the Japanese command and the way in which the landing at Hollandia had been meticulously planned. If the Japanese had kept their troops at Hollandia, the fight for the airdromes could have lasted for months.[6]

As the Reckless Task Force made their three-pronged landings at Hollandia, the Persecution Task Force, made up primarily of the 163rd Regiment, stormed the beaches of Aitape nearly eighty miles away. The Task Force's objective was the Tadji Airdrome and the associated landing strips.

Planes launched from carriers covered the approach of the LCIs (Landing Craft Infantry) carrying the men of the 163rd to the beaches of Aitape which had been bombarded by U.S. Navy rocket boats just before they arrived.[7] Even combat veterans like Doyle Bruce and Jack Anderson were awed by the amount and variety of men an equipment devoted to the landings at Hollandia and Aitape. Bruce counted 109 ships involved in the mission.[8] The ships they traveled on also carried new military vehicles, primarily two different types of amphibious landing craft.[9] Anderson felt the invasion armada must have contained at least one of every type of ship in the U.S. Navy and could not help but contrast the landing craft that would take Company G to the beaches at Aitape with the makeshift rafts and captured boats they had used on the Kumusi patrol. The Naval bombardment of the company's landing area impressed him as well.[10]

In the predawn hours of April 22, 1943, the men of Company G went over the side of the troopships that had carried them from Finschhafen to Aitape, climbed down the rough cargo nets, and boarded the LCIs that would carry them to the beaches in the second wave to go in at Aitape. By the time the landing craft carrying the 3rd Battalion headed

Members of the 163rd on board a Landing Craft Infantry (LCI) carrying them to the beaches of Aitape, April 22, 1944. (National Archives)

for the beach the sun was up and the sky was a bright blue. As the first wave chugged towards the beach, 2nd Battalion's landing craft swung away from their troop transports and began circling in place, waiting for the order to go in themselves. The men, with their packs laden with equipment and supplies, were jammed into the landing crafts so tightly that when the order came to fix bayonets, each man had to affix the bayonet of the man next to him because they could not reach their own. For the inexperienced Westerfield, who had joined the company so late that he had never even had any training in amphibious beach landings, the long time he spent packed shoulder to shoulder with other men onboard the landing craft that would take him to the beach heightened his anxiety about combat.[11]

The regiment made the landing on time and faced almost no resistance. The regiment's 3rd Battalion hit the beach first followed by the 2nd Battalion under a barrage of naval artillery that lit up the jungle and the beaches beyond them. The only real problem with the landing resulted from the navy sending the regiment ashore on a beach a thousand yards from the beaches designated for their landing. This led to some initial confusion, but the mistake was discovered and worked through without too much time lost.[12] Most of the company reached the beach and crossed to the cover of the jungle unscathed because the naval bombardment had reduced the Japanese defensive positions and chased the survivors away from the beaches. Baird's squad landed on the extreme left flank of Company G. His platoon's veteran lieutenant had injured his leg while trying to board one of the landing craft during a training exercise the night before the attack, so Baird and the other platoon sergeants shared leadership responsibilities for much of the Aitape operation.[13] Company G's weapons platoon drew enemy rifle fire when they landed and one member of that group was wounded. Across the beach and into the jungle the men of Company G stopped to repack their equipment to make marching easier and to make themselves more combat ready before heading for their next objective.[14] Baird's squad faced no opposition but passed through an area where Japanese buildings had been destroyed that contained several dead enemy soldiers and a few stunned survivors.[15] When 3rd Platoon's landing craft reached the beach at Aitape and pulled up onto the sand, Westerfield felt like the ramp in front of him would never drop open. When it did, he leapt from the boat and fell into the wet sand which filled the muzzle of his rifle. He rose and ran across the beach stopping in a field of kunai grass with the rest of the company. He stopped to rearrange his pack and to clear his rifle of sand then rose with the rest of his platoon and began to move forward.[16]

The 163rd marched inland from the beach still encountering few enemy soldiers. The Japanese forces had retreated to the west during the naval bombardment, allowing the Americans to move unhindered. 2nd Battalion proceeded cautiously inland to the Tadji airdromes. The large Japanese force they expected to oppose them never materialized and neither did the tree snipers that had plagued the battalion's early days

A soldier of the 163rd Infantry Regiment waits on the beach at Aitape for orders to move forward. Note that the soldier carries an M1 Carbine. The variety of weapons available to the soldiers in the Pacific increased after the fight for Buna–Sanananda–Gona. (National Archives)

on the Sanananda Road.[17] The men of Company G plunged into the dense jungle utilizing any trail they could find, emerging on a compressed gravel road near a Japanese mess kitchen that appeared to have just been abandoned. As they labored through the jungle, Westerfield thought he saw a Japanese soldier moving parallel to them and prepared to open fire.

A Company G veteran stopped him. The man he thought was a Japanese soldier was an American. Fortunately, company veterans had arranged their line of advance so that one of them was in front and one behind each pair of rookies. The sound of machine-gun fire nearby drove the men to ground, but it was not the Japanese. An American soldier had decided to search for souvenirs and was mistaken for a Japanese soldier. He sustained multiple gunshot wounds but lived. The incident, at least temporarily, discouraged other GIs from souvenir hunting. After the firing stopped, Company G rose and continued toward the Tadji airdrome and found it abandoned.[18] The 163rd had landed at 6:30 that morning and by 1:00 p.m. they had accomplished their first day's primary objective. The army engineers were already at work on the landing strips to make them capable of handling the planes of the 78th Fighter Wing of the RAAF which would make Aitape their new base.[19]

When Company G reached the Tadji drome they received orders to dig in and wait for artillery to be brought up to cover their next advance.

Elements of the 163rd wade onto the beach at Aitape, where smoke rises from Japanese structures destroyed by naval bombardment that preceded the landing. (National Archives).

Much to the amusement of veterans in the company, who only dug rudimentary foxholes for themselves, Westerfield dutifully dug a nearly perfect foxhole with the flimsy trenching tool that was a part of every infantryman's equipment. The work left him tired, drenched in sweat, and thirsty. When battalion command ordered the company to proceed with the next phase of their mission Westerfield understood why the veterans had laughed at his efforts and only dug shallow foxholes.

As Company G moved inland, the terrain became increasingly swampy. After exerting energy digging foxholes in the hot and humid atmosphere of New Guinea, most of the men had very little water in their canteens. Still the company moved quickly against no opposition to capture a fighter plane landing strip associated with the Tadji airdrome. They continued on, crossing creeks, flooded land, and rivers on log trails and bridges made by the Japanese and arrived at their phase one final objective by 1:00 the afternoon of the Aitape D-Day. As Westerfield and the rest of Company G marched deeper into the swampy jungles of New Guinea, water became a problem. Each man carried a single canteen as a part of their standard equipment and some, like Westerfield, also carried extra equipment. It was Westerfield's bad luck to be the carrier of the platoon's collapsible grenade launcher along with five heavy shells in his pack. As the heat rose and the water ran short many members of his platoon began to shed equipment they found unnecessary. Westerfield chose his gas mask and threw it in a river during a crossing.

Company G made camp the first night at an old mission where they dug two-man trenches to create a perimeter. When the trenches were dug, the pickets were called in and GIs in pairs settled in for their first night. Each pair had the responsibility of keeping watch through the night. Westerfield took the first watch. All through his watch his imagination worked to convince him that every shadow, every rustle, every twig snap was a Japanese soldier sneaking up on his position. On one occasion he was so sure an enemy soldier was approaching that he nearly pulled the pin and threw a grenade. When his watch was over, he fell asleep quickly but was awakened by his partner after what seemed like only a few minutes. His partner claimed he was falling asleep on watch and told Westerfield he had to take watch again. Westerfield was not irritated by this. His ability to stand watch and keep his comrades safe made him feel like he was contributing.[20]

The next morning the company marched deeper into the jungle till they reached the Raihu River and made camp for the second night. They again established a perimeter and dug trenches, but few of the men got any sleep. Sand crabs came out all around their position and the sounds of their scuttling convinced more than one man on watch to lob his grenade in the direction of what they believed were approaching Japanese soldiers. In company lore that night became known as "The Battle of Raihu River."

The morning after the fight against the sand crabs Company G rose and once again headed into the jungles around Aitape. They marched to the Aitape River which they crossed on the remnants of a partially destroyed bridge. Evidence of Japanese defenses were all around them as they moved up a hill towards Aitape village, but they only encountered two Japanese soldiers who the company scouts found having breakfast in an abandoned Australian jungle hospital. The scouts killed one of the men but the other escaped. As the men marched on to the site of their next base of operations on Windy Point, their appreciation for the plans made by General MacArthur increased. The Japanese defenses on the ridge were well constructed and densely packed. If not for MacArthur fooling the Japanese into believing the U.S. attack would take place at Wewak those positions would have been manned by a large Japanese garrison and the fight for Aitape might have taken a month and cost many American lives. Company G remained at Windy Point, patrolling the jungle during the day, and sleeping inside a defensive perimeter at night, until they were relieved by a company from the 32nd Division.[21]

While on patrol in an around Aitape Bruce gained more insight into the Japanese treatment of the natives of New Guinea and collected a few souvenirs. Aitape was a part of Dutch New Guinea and home to a lot of coconut plantations. When the Japanese took over the region they imprisoned some of the native population and put them to work gathering fibers from the coconuts and making rope and other things from it. While exploring the area on patrol Bruce and his comrades discovered a Japanese lookout station high on a bluff overlooking the ocean complete with a high-powered telescope and a radio. From that station the Japanese could observe the movement of allied ships and report them to their high command. Bruce and the other men of his company found some money, Dutch guilders, some of which they kept as souvenirs. But Bruce's most prized souvenir was a Japanese flag he found in a hidden cave the Japanese were using for a hideout. He kept that flag with him for the duration of the war and recorded the date and place of all of the 163rd's actions on it.[22]

Despite the limited presence of Japanese forces around Aitape all of Company G's patrols in the area were dangerous and some were deadly. On a short patrol to search for indigenous people negatively affected by enemy activity Anderson's squad came under enemy fire as they attempted to cross a small river. The men who had already made it across jumped in the water and attempted to swim to safety. A rifle bullet killed one of those men and another GI who was providing covering fire had a bullet graze the side of his forehead. The wound bled in gushes with each of the man's heartbeats. Anderson and others tried to apply a pressure bandage but could only stop the bleeding by pressing a thumb to the wound. Because they had no stretcher the man had to walk back to Company G's perimeter where there was a field hospital, with another man walking beside him using his thumb to stop the bleeding. There Anderson watched as the surgeon struggled to tie off the artery that had been damaged while blood spurted out. Despite his experience in combat the sight made Anderson feel sick.[23]

Not all of Company G's patrols involved finding and destroying the enemy. On one patrol Bruce Baird's squad escorted an Australian official and a young interpreter who could speak the language of the indigenous population as they moved around Aitape in search of indigenous groups that needed help. The Japanese had destroyed many of their villages and many of these people needed food and medical help. Baird's squad and other elements of Company G escorted them to a large camp run by the Australian government where they could get the help they needed.[24]

Only an advanced company of the 3rd Battalion met any significant resistance during the Aitape action. While patrolling in the hills near Kamti village a company from the 127th Regiment, which was part of the 32nd Division that also took part in the landings at Aitape, made contact with a large Japanese force on the trail near the village. A vicious firefight ensued during which U.S. heavy machine guns killed dozens of Japanese soldiers. A company from the 163rd's 3rd Battalion moved to support them and both groups were cut off from the rest of the American forces when the Japanese force moved to surround them. During the night Japanese soldiers gathered at the base of the hill in preparation for an attack. The GIs threw and rolled grenades down the hill into their ranks. The American command had to fly supplies into the men trapped in a hilltop village. In the morning, the Japanese attacked, but the Americans fought them off. More Japanese soldiers began arriving and preparing for a third attack, but before it took place, both the company from the 127th and the 163rd were able to withdraw.[25]

Like most of the rest of the 163rd Regiment, 2nd Battalion achieved all of its objectives without major enemy engagements. The companies that made up the battalion settled into their defensive perimeters and spent most of the rest of their time patrolling the jungles of Aitape looking for enemy units retreating through the area or attempting to link up with other elements of the Japanese army elsewhere in New Guinea.[26]

On May 2, all the scattered elements of Company G were gathered together and transported up the coast in LCIs to make a surprise landing near Serroe village. Heavy machine guns and 81mm mortars of Company H, as well as guides from the Australian Army, supported Company G's move.

Company G's second beach landing was a mess. The coxswains of their landing craft dropped the ramps to the boats on a submerged sandbar twenty-five yards from the beach. In some places the men were forced to wade through deep water. At others, the men stepped off the ramps into deep water and got caught up in cross currents. Weighed down by their heavy packs, several men began to drown. Other Company G men jumped in to help them. They saved all of the men they saw struggling. One member of the company was dragged under a landing boat and drowned though the men of the company would not know that for some time. They were lucky that the Japanese did not have troops in the area to defend the beach or things could have been much worse.

The company moved to Serroe village, meeting only light opposition and killing two Japanese soldiers, before reaching the village where they set up their perimeter. Despite the limited contact with the enemy, the men knew the Japanese were in the area. Each morning platoons from Company G went out on patrol expecting a fight. A patrol found and killed two enemy soldiers and so did another patrol the next day. They found evidence of recent Japanese military activity, but the main Japanese force had withdrawn before the GIs arrived.[27]

Once Anderson's platoon landed and Company G's combat objectives had been accomplished, his experiences at Aitape settled into a routine of daily combat patrols and nights spent at various encampments. During a break at one river crossing, the men stopped to cool their feet in a river causing their native carriers and guides a great deal of distress. The natives kept pointing to the river and repeating, "pauk pauk." The GIs did not know what they were saying and only later learned that "pauk pauk" was their word for crocodile. Company G had a "pauk pauk" as a mascot after catching a six-foot crocodile. The mascot did not last long. The company commanding officer made them set the crocodile free shortly after learning about it.

After the company's move to Serroe village, Anderson received orders to take his platoon on a nighttime patrol inside the area the regiment occupied to clean out any Japanese soldiers located between the perimeters of the individual companies. Anderson understood the danger involved in such a mission. At night, operating within the American perimeter filled with nervous GIs likely to lob a grenade at any sound, not to mention the likelihood of meeting with enemy soldiers, the mission seemed like certain death. He refused to follow the order even at one point suggesting that his commanding officer come and lead the patrol himself. That same officer told Anderson that he did not have a choice. It was a nervous, but effective night. The patrol managed to avoid American grenades and at the same time cleared the American area of remaining Japanese soldiers. Following that patrol Anderson went to his commanding officer Lieutenant Buck Braman and asked to apply for a commission. Anderson eventually received his appointment to the rank of Second Lieutenant on August 1, 1944.[28]

By the time the Hollandia and Aitape missions were being planned the U.S. Army in the Pacific was beginning to benefit from U.S. industrial power. Jack Anderson catalogued all the versions of landing and support craft they now had available to them. The variety and the specific purpose and construction of each impressed him. There were amphibious personnel assault vehicles capable of carrying hundreds of men and all their equipment from ship to shore, Landing Craft Infantry that could carry a whole company, and smaller landing craft mounted with .50 caliber machine guns. Most impressive were the huge landing craft tank ships that could carry tanks and trucks, and which had big doors at the bow that swung open and created a ramp that allowed tanks to drive directly from the ship to the beach. They had come a long way from the salvaged Japanese landing boats and improvised rafts that Company G had used during the Kumusi patrol.[29]

Company G remained at Serroe village until they were relieved on May 7 by a company from the 126th Regiment. They boarded landing boats and traveled to Saint Ana Plantation where they rejoined the rest of the 163rd Regiment.[30]

For soldiers in a combat zone there is always the potential for danger whether the enemy is present or not. An incident that occurred during the end of the regiment's time in the Aitape vicinity reminded the men that despite the relative lack of action, they were in a dangerous business. In preparation for the regiment's next move, Company H conducted a training exercise for some of the new mortar crews that had arrived after the end of major combat operations in the area. They set up six mortars on a piece of flat ground very close together so that the new crew men could better see the effects of mortar shells falling in a group. Army regulations demanded that there be thirty feet between mortars for training purposes but there was less than ten feet between each of the crews. When the command to fire was given, all six mortar crews fired their weapons. Five shells arched over the nearby jungle and exploded. The sixth detonated just as it left the mortar tube. Seven men were killed, and dozens wounded in the explosion. Company H lost half of its mortar crews. It was the kind of incident that cast a pall over the men and marred what had been a successful and relatively low-cost military action.[31]

CHAPTER 8

Wakde

May 17, 1944–May 26, 1944

One of the benefits of the triangular infantry divisions adopted by the U.S. Army during World War II was the ability of each of the three regiments within a division to act independently, as regimental combat teams, to carry out separate missions that built upon one another. MacArthur had used this feature during the 41st Division's Hollandia–Aitape operations during which the 162nd Regimental Combat Team and the 186th Regimental Combat Team acted together to take Hollandia and the 163rd Regimental Combat Team acted alone to take Aitape. This feature would be utilized again and in much the same way for the U.S. Army's invasion of the strategically important island of Biak. But before landings at Biak could take place, the Japanese airfields on the small island of Wakde had to be taken.[1]

The island of Wakde (also known as Insoemoar) consisted of a few square miles of coral- and jungle-covered land just a few miles off the coast of New Guinea. During their occupation of the island, the Japanese constructed an impressive airfield complete with a control tower and airplane hangars. This made it a valuable target for U.S. military planners who knew that it would serve as a valuable allied air base during the invasion of Biak and later the southern Philippines. The 163rd Regimental Combat Team under the command of General Jens A. Doe was selected to make the attack on the Toem area of New Guinea, across from Wakde, and then Wakde itself. The 163rd made up the infantry element of the Tornado Task Force which also included the 167th and 218th Field Artillery battalions and other support groups. The task force would also have the assistance of the U.S. Navy that provided the landing craft and the crews who operated them.

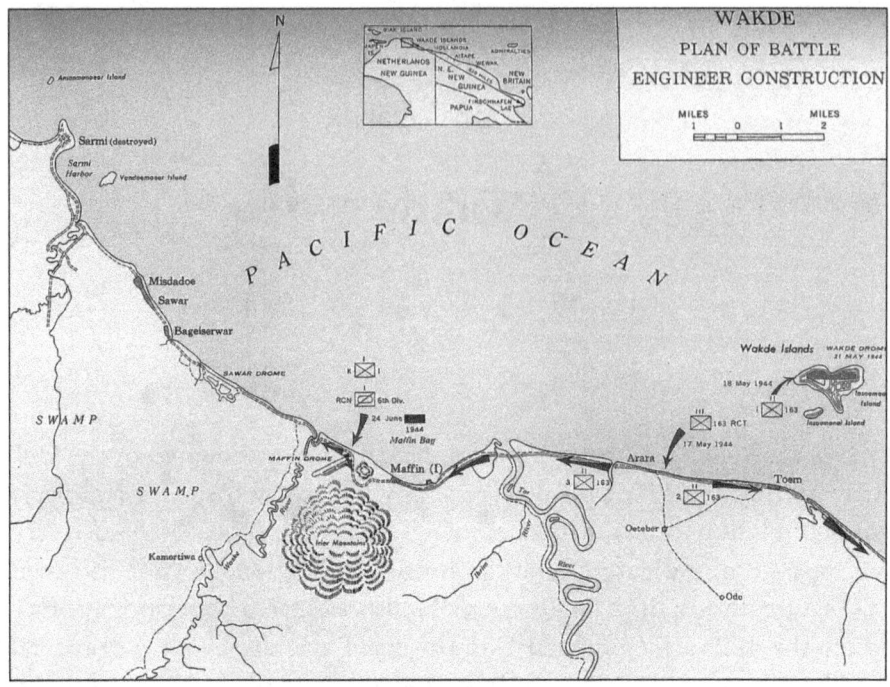

This map shows the 163rd's landing at Arare, 2nd Battalion's advance towards Toem, and 1st Battalion's attack on the island of Wakde. (U.S. Army Center of Military History)

The plan for the attack involved a landing on the New Guinea mainland near Arara by the 3rd and 2nd Battalions to establish a base of operations for the 1st Battalion's attack on Wakde itself the next day.

A naval bombardment of the Arara landing area preceded the landing craft carrying the 2nd and 3rd Battalions to the beach on the morning of May 17. The 3rd Battalion landed first securing the beachhead followed closely by the 2nd Battalion which moved through the 3rd Battalion positions and then east towards Toem village. The 3rd Battalion continued to secure the beach before moving west toward the Tor River to guard the right flank of the 1st Battalions landing. When the 1st hit the beaches, they followed the 2nd Battalion towards Toem. There, along with the Field Artillery battalions, they set up a firebase to help cover the landings on Wakde scheduled for the next day. Neither the 2nd nor 3rd Battalions faced much resistance from the Japanese military on May 17.[2]

As a part of the 2nd Battalion that landed on the New Guinea mainland across from Wakde the day before the invasion of the island itself, Company G's part in the battle for Wakde proved comparatively easy. They were a part of the second wave that landed near Arara after the 3rd Battalion and then turned east towards Toem village.[3] The landing itself was made more difficult by the presence of tanks that had not been properly balanced on the landing craft that caused the vessels to plunge to the right after cresting each wave. The extra motion made more than one member of Company G sick.[4] On the approach to Toem, Company G scouts encountered and killed a single Japanese soldier. Hargis Westerfield hoped for a chance to fire his rifle, but the men were ordered not to fire for fear of hitting an American GI. A Company G patrol probing the jungle outside Toem in the area of Tementoe Creek found a squad of fifteen enemy soldiers and killed them all. Afterwards the company moved into an area along Tementoe Creek and dug in along its banks. For several nights small groups of Japanese soldiers attacked or tried to sneak through or past Company G's perimeter. For Westerfield these were long tense nights. On one night the company's position received a bombardment of Japanese mortar shells that were all duds. On another a Japanese non-com and an officer tried to wade across Tementoe Creek near his position but were cut down by a Company G BAR man. His machine gun burst killed one of the men but only wounded the other who began to moan and cry out in the pitch-black darkness. Most of the other Company G men on guard had no problem letting the wounded man suffer, but when he called out something in English it angered Westerfield. He woke his sergeant who threw a grenade in the direction of the wounded Japanese soldier and killed him. Like the Japanese officer and sergeant, most of the Japanese who approached the American position were killed without any American casualties. When one of the company's BAR men died in an early morning attack by a group of Japanese soldiers, reprisals came quickly. The company formed a squad that attacked the area of the jungle from which the enemy fire had come and killed four. These small encounters continued through the days and nights that followed.[5]

As the landing at Arara was under way, scouting parties in landing craft that were no longer needed surveyed a small island off the coast of Wakde called Insoemanai and found no enemy presence there. Company D of the 1st Battalion, along with the 163rd's heavy weapons company, rushed to secure the island as well as establish machine gun and mortar positions from which they could also provide fire support during the Wakde landings. Those positions played a crucial role in the fight for Wakde.

In the lead up to the attack on Wakde, Allied air forces had flown over the island for ten days. Allied command reported no Japanese antiaircraft activity on any of their flyovers. This led to the widespread belief that the island was only lightly defended. American commanders felt confident that what defenses and defenders the island did contain would be largely destroyed by a sustained bombardment. Beginning almost twenty-four hours before the scheduled landing, Allied forces including bomber planes, field artillery, naval vessels, mortars and machine guns subjected Wakde to sustained bombardment which continued until the first waves of men from the 1st Battalion were within a few hundred yards of the beach.[6] For the men waiting on the beaches at Toem the ferocity of the bombardment of Wakde which began the night before the invasion and continued as they loaded into their landing craft and chugged toward the island raised their hopes for an easy landing. Reports that Wakde was mostly unoccupied further reduced the fear and anxiety of hitting the beaches. Thirty-six bombers flew over and dropped their payloads on the island as the long-range guns of two destroyers accompanied the steady fire of the field artillery that pounded the small island. To the men in the landing craft, it seemed impossible that anything could live through that bombardment, and they became even more confident.[7]

Companies A, B, C, and F (the latter from 2nd Battalion) approached the beaches of Wakde in six waves of LCMs (Landing Craft Mechanized). Company A and F were to hit the beach abreast of one another, secure the landing areas, then turn in opposite directions from one another, one moving left and the other right, as companies B and C landed behind them and moved inland to capture the airstrip. Successive waves of support units including engineers were to follow closely behind and begin work on the airstrip as soon as possible. That was not what happened.

As the first wave of LCMs approached the island and the allied bombing and shelling let up, Japanese machine gun and mortar fire began to zero in on the landing craft and the GIs inside them. Clearly the Japanese

Men of the 1st Battalion of the 163rd on the beach near Arare preparing for the attack on Wakde, May 18, 1944. (National Archives)

soldiers on Wakde were not all dead and intended to fight.[8] The coxswain of one of the landing craft and two crew members died in the hail of machine gun and rifle bullets, and though some of the men on board attempted to steer the craft to the landing area it veered off course and crashed into Insoemanai island temporarily preventing those men from joining the fighting. The lead landing craft's coxswain was also killed along with a member of 1st Battalion who took a bullet in the neck. A bullet tore through the mouth of another man knocking out his teeth. Blood and water mixed in the bottom of several landing craft and sloshed around the ankles of the men of 1st Battalion.[9]

The beach offered less cover than the landing craft and casualties among the first wave of Americans rose steadily. As succeeding waves of GIs arrived on the beach, protection from the Japanese mortar,

Soldiers of the 163rd 1st Battalion pinned down and stacked up on the beach at Wakde, May 18, 1944. (National Archives)

machine gun, and rifle fire was hard to find. The men stacked up behind what little cover there was. The heavy weapons company and Company D, with their machine guns and mortars, poured bullets and shells into the Japanese positions from nearby Insoemanai island which prevented the Japanese from organizing a counterattack and probably saved the lives of many of the men on Wakde's beaches. Gradually individual men or men in small groups began to maneuver into firing positions and return fire. Progress was slow and casualties were high until the LCT (landing craft tanks) carrying three Sherman tanks arrived at the beach head. The first tank to roll down the ramp of an LCT disappeared in the surf with only its turret above water. It would later be towed out and participate in the fight for Wakde on the second day. The two other tanks made it safely to the beach and went directly into action, firing their cannons and machine guns.

Sherman tanks and their crews on the beach at Arare after being unloaded from Landing Ship Tanks (LST). Three of these tanks would play key roles in the fight for Wakde on May 18 and May 19, 1943. (National Archives)

The Japanese had no weapons capable of destroying or disabling the tanks, but individual soldiers tried anyway.[10] One Japanese soldier charged directly at one of the tanks and fired his rifle down the muzzle of its canon. When this had no effect, he climbed on top of the tank to either get into the tank or to drop a grenade into the turret. A wave of American rifle bullets cut him down.[11] With the help of the tanks the GIs secured the beach head in another fifteen minutes of fighting.

Despite their effectiveness these two tanks could not aid and cover all the advancing American companies. Command tried to send them to the places they felt enemy defenses would be toughest and advancing would be the most difficult. The tanks helped Company A take a low ridge on the east end of the island where it was thought the Japanese would have many men and defensive positions, but that proved not to be true. The tanks traversed the island to help company B whose advance to the airstrip had been stopped by long-range rifle and machine-gun fire. Then they moved to the left of the American line to help Company F which was encountering fierce resistance from enemy soldiers who occupied a piece of high ground. At different times the tanks joined squads from Company B and Company C to help them break through to the airstrip as well. After several hours of combat, the tank commander informed the company commanders that the tanks would have to return to the beachhead to get more ammunition.

The chaos at the beachhead did not help with the resupply of the tanks. Because of the difficult landing, good communication with all the landing craft headed for Wakde could not be established. As a result, equipment, soldiers, and service units crowded the beach. To add to this already confusing scene, Company D arrived from their position on Insoemanai to reinforce the other units of 1st Battalion.

Company commanders resumed their attacks without the support of the tanks and were able to cut off and surround a group of about one hundred Japanese soldiers. Most of these soldiers were killed by the GIs, but a few chose to commit suicide instead. On another part of the island, Company B still faced tough opposition and had failed to keep up with the line of the other companies as they advanced. This created a gap in the American line that made it possible for the Japanese to redeploy across the island and even created the opportunity for them to attack the American beachhead. Alerted to the danger by the Japanese attack, Battalion command moved Companies A, C, and F into positions adjacent to Company B which created a perimeter that trapped the Japanese between them and the sea. Small pockets of enemy soldiers continued to cause problems outside the American perimeter, but as darkness approached, the men of 1st Battalion dug defensive positions in which to pass the night.

That night on Wakde did not pass quietly. Japanese mortars fired shells at the American positions, but they were silenced by returning mortar fire. In the hours after midnight, a Japanese squad snuck through the American perimeter down an unused side road. As they approached the Battalion HQ, an alert machine gunner on guard duty heard them and gunned down fourteen of the fifteen men. The survivor was the only prisoner that the Americans took during the fight for Wakde. Elsewhere a group of fifty-four Japanese who had evaded the GIs gathered and launched a predawn attack on a unit of engineers on the beach. The engineers defended their position well and, under the leadership of a sergeant, launched a counterattack that wiped out the enemy.[12] All along the American perimeter Japanese soldiers attacked alone or in small groups.[13] By morning Company A alone had killed around eighty Japanese soldiers trying to break through the American lines.[14]

After a delay caused by the attack on the engineers, which made the tanks late to get into position, the coordinated American attack on the Japanese resumed and went well. By noon the 163rd controlled the entire island, but Japanese soldiers remained and fought on from deep coral caves where the weapons of the tanks could not reach them. Flamethrowers were brought forward to kill the Japanese in the caves while the last remaining pocket of enemy soldiers on the north end of the island were eliminated. By 5:00 p.m. the battle for Wakde had ended and the units of the 1st Battalion settled in for a rest. They had met and dealt with unexpectedly fierce resistance. An inspection of the island revealed that in addition to constructing an airstrip, hangers, and a control tower, the Japanese had dug numerous defensive bunkers deep into the coral. It was in these defensive positions that the Japanese soldiers had survived the bombardment that preceded the 163rd's landing on Wakde. The successful conquest of the island cost the U.S. Army the lives of twenty men and thirty-six were wounded. Japanese losses included 803 of the 804 military personnel on Wakde. In the days after the fighting ended, U.S. intelligence learned that one part of the Japanese force defending Wakde was a company of "Tiger Marines" who had taken part in the "Rape of Nanking." The men of the 163rd took pride in having destroyed that unit.[15]

In the days following the landings at Toem and 1st Battalions conquest of Wakde, one thing improved for the men of Company G—the food. A cook assigned to the company mess figured out that he could obtain fresh baking supplies as well as better canned foods by trading Japanese souvenirs with crews from the navy ships offshore for those items.[16] But those days also saw Company G and the rest of the 2nd Battalion

Medics treat a wounded soldier of the 163rd Regiment on the beach at Wakde, May 18, 1944. (National Archives)

engaged in aggressive and deadly combat patrols in the jungles around Toem and Tementoe Creek. These patrols led to fire fights with small and sometimes large groups of Japanese soldiers who were seeking to make it through the American lines to join other Japanese units further west or to get to the coast and hope for naval evacuation. Company G met and killed eleven such enemy soldiers on May 24 but lost an Indonesian guide attached to their unit from the Netherland Indonesian Colonial Administration. On May 26 a Company G patrol of forty men moved to a position on Tementoe Creek for the purpose of drawing Japanese attacks. Following a brief machine gun battle with a group of Japanese troops, the Company G patrol moved through Masi Masi village and found numerous prepared Japanese defensive positions but no Japanese soldiers.[17]

The presence of Javanese men who spoke Dutch because of the time they had spent working for the Dutch government in Northern

New Guinea proved to be very helpful to the American GIs in the Toem–Wakde area. They made it possible for Company G patrols to gather information from the Indigenous population, sometimes acted as scouts patrolling ahead of Company G squads and were the key to the success of humanitarian missions to help find indigenous groups and help them flee from the Japanese army.[18]

The time spent patrolling around Toem gave Jack Anderson several new combat experiences. During a period of aggressive patrolling, the platoon that Anderson led was assigned to retrieve a telephone wire that had earlier been laid through the jungle to create an efficient communications link between units. Headquarters worried that if the wire was not picked up it could lead the Japanese directly to the American defensive positions. On a well-trafficked trail Anderson's platoon scouts discovered a group of Japanese soldiers resting and eating in a clearing. Anderson hooked a phone to the line that his group was retrieving and called in a request for reinforcements. In the meantime, he positioned his men in the jungle along the trail to create an ambush. When the Japanese soldiers ended their meal and continued down the trail, they walked right into the trap that Anderson had laid for them. He waited for the last man to pass his position, then stepped out of the jungle and killed him, which was the signal for his men to open fire. All the Japanese soldiers were killed. It was Anderson's first planned ambush and a successful one.

On another patrol during which Anderson's platoon roamed far from the American defensive position, they encountered a group of enemy soldiers on the trail between themselves and the American lines. Anderson called back to 2nd Battalion on the radio and requested an artillery strike to wipe out the enemy. The newly emplaced 105 Howitzers within 2nd Battalion perimeter answered with a barrage that destroyed the Japanese position. This was Anderson's first experience in coordinating an artillery attack with the actions of his own infantry group.

Anderson's next new experience was almost his last. The 163rd took advantage of the large number of available landing craft in the Wakde area to speed up and increase the range of its patrols. Platoons were transported to areas that they were assigned to patrol by these landing craft. The LCIs would let them off and pick them up along the beach. Because the landing craft were part of the U.S. Navy their onboard radios and the GI's radios were not able to communicate effectively, so the men worked out a simple system of signals using smoke grenades. When a platoon completed its patrol and was ready to be evacuated, a soldier would walk out onto the beach and set off a white smoke grenade. If the platoon needed reinforcements, they would detonate a red smoke grenade. At the end of one of the patrols that Anderson led he walked out onto the beach thinking he had a white smoke grenade in his hand. He pulled the pin and threw it a few yards away. Instead of the small pop of a smoke grenade there was the loud explosion of the white phosphorus grenade he had picked up by mistake. White phosphorus shrapnel and smoke surrounded him. The rest of his platoon assumed he had been killed. On a reflex Anderson had turned and jumped into a water-filled coral crater near where he stood. The next thing he knew, his men were pulling him out of the crater. Miraculously not a single piece of phosphorus had wounded Anderson or even burned any of his clothing.[19]

On May 30, a large-scale Japanese attack caught most of the 163rd Regiment, now reunited on the New Guinea mainland near Wakde, off guard. Regimental command believed the only substantial enemy force was to the west of the regiment's position, and as a result, the men of 1st and 3rd Battalions had pitched tents and strung hammocks in which to sleep at night. Only 2nd Battalion remained dug in. At dusk more than 200 Japanese soldiers hit and penetrated the regiment's perimeter. Groups of Japanese soldiers made it all the way to regimental HQ and the motor pool where soldiers, who were technically not combat soldiers, had to pick up their weapons and fight for their lives. In all the 163rd lost ten soldiers in the Japanese surprise attack and had twelve other men wounded. Being an experienced and battle-hardened military unit helped the 163rd to quickly organize for defense and counterattack. That experience and the bravery of soldiers in the motor pool, engineering units, and even the headquarters unit, prevented a disaster for the regiment.[20]

With the Japanese air bases at Wakde secured and ready to accommodate allied planes, the next phase of MacArthur's plan could get underway.

CHAPTER 9

Biak

May 27, 1944–February 27, 1945

When Jack Anderson first caught site of Biak from the rolling deck of the landing craft taking him to the island all he could think about was how much the near-vertical coral cliffs and ridges that overlooked the beaches resembled saw teeth stacked row-upon-row and what an awful place it would be to fight. Though his unit arrived well after the initial assault on Biak, he would have plenty of time to find out just how difficult combat there would be.[1]

Biak is one of the two Schouten Islands that lie off the northwest coast of Dutch New Guinea. Covered by scrub jungle, the interior of the island was not a conducive location for large scale military action. But along the coast, separated from the interior jungle by sharp high coral cliffs and ridges, there were pockets of flat, stable land capable of supporting air bases. The Japanese had three such bases on Biak in 1944. These bases made it a target for MacArthur's drive toward the Philippines and the key step in his plans to invade those islands.[2]

In fact, Biak was the key to a surprising number of Allied plans for the war in the Pacific in the Summer of 1944. Not only did MacArthur need the island's airfields to give him the bomber support to attack the Japanese in the Philippines, establishment of Allied air bases on Biak could also give air cover to the navy's planned invasion of the Marianas Islands to the East. In addition, taking Biak would effectively stop a planned Japanese effort to reinforce their positions in western New Guinea, which the Allies had learned about as a result of successful codebreaking. For all these reasons, MacArthur decided to

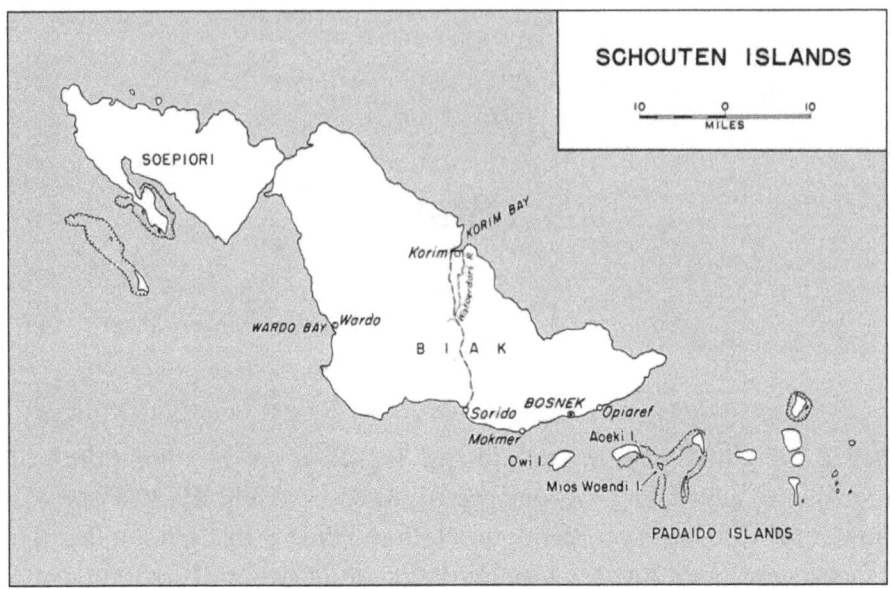

Map of the Schouten Islands. (U.S. Army Center of Military History)

gamble on an attempt to seize Biak in a rapid move over considerable distance. The 163rd's capture of Wakde made the attempt to take Biak possible. The airfields of Wakde provided the Biak invasion force with the fighter and bomber cover needed to make the leap of hundreds of miles. With that support MacArthur hoped for a quick victory at Biak, but in his rush to capture the Island he underestimated enemy strength and failed to appreciate how the island's difficult terrain and lack of available water would impact the GIs sent to take it.[3]

The Hurricane Task Force, consisting of the 162nd and 186th Regimental Combat Teams, began preparation for the invasion of Biak even before the 163rd's landings at Wakde. The 163rd Regimental Combat Team would remain at Wakde to guard the island against any Japanese counterattack and to act as a reserve unit for the attacking regiments.[4] The 162nd and 186th had remained at Hollandia following their successful surprise attack that launched Allied forces hundreds of miles up the New Guinea Coast and isolated the large Japanese garrison at Wewak. On May 25, both regiments assembled on the beaches where they had landed weeks before and boarded troopships for Biak.

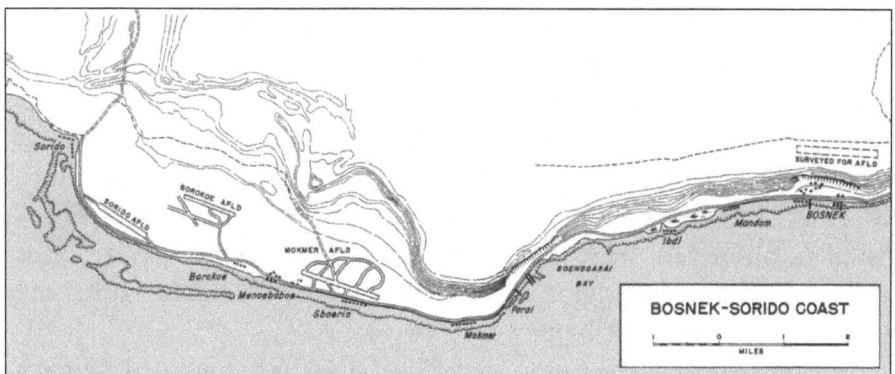

Map showing the area of Biak between Mokmer and Bosnek in which the 41st Infantry, including the 163rd Regiment's Company G, engaged the enemy beginning in May of 1944. (U.S. Army Center of Military History)

Allied planes and ships had been bombing and bombarding the island consistently in the days and weeks leading up to the Hurricane Task Force's planned landings. On May 27, a forty-minute naval bombardment and aerial bombing lit up the coastal areas of Biak near Bosnek. The planes and shells flew over the heads of the landing craft carrying the 2nd Battalion of the 186th as they rushed toward the beach in the first wave of the attack. Thick smoke from the bombardments severely limited visibility for the men driving the landing craft and that combined with a strong current running parallel to the beach, caused them to miss the landing zone by two miles. This delayed the establishment of a secure beachhead by both the 2nd and the 3rd Battalions of the 186th, but neither unit met much resistance.

The 162nd's 2nd and 3rd Battalions followed the 186th to the beaches at Bosnek and then moved west through their position, along the beach toward Mokmer, the location of the largest and most important Japanese airfield several miles away. The missed landing zone and the confusion caused when one unit moved through the position of another delayed the 162nd's move at a time when speed was needed. As the 162nd neared the village of Parai, the coral ridges and cliffs rose high above them and crowded out toward the beach creating a narrow defile where they encountered significant Japanese resistance. Tanks were brought forward from the beachhead to knock out the lightly defended Japanese position on the cliffs.

While the 162nd worked its way toward Mokmer, the 186th extended the beachhead at Bosnek and sent patrols north to scout access to the island's internal plateau. They met only light resistance. In the meantime, other elements of the Hurricane Task Force made their landings at Bosnek. These included the 205th and 146th Field Artillery Battalions, the 121st Field Artillery from the 32nd Division, the 947th Field Artillery Battalion of the 6th Army which brought 105mm Howitzers, as well as tanks and their crews, engineers, and medical personnel. The Hurricane Task Force did not lack firepower.

On day two of the invasion of Biak, the 162nd continued its push toward the Mokmer airfields with the 3rd Battalion in the lead, followed by the 2nd Battalion with the 1st following in reserve. At a point just east of Mokmer village where a cliff jutted out to the ocean, the Japanese launched an attack that divided the 3rd Battalion from the 2nd. Sustained fire from the Japanese position pinned the 2nd Battalion down and it was unable to fight its way past to rejoin the 3rd Battalion, which was sustaining significant casualties. The Japanese positions high on the cliffs were hidden from the Americans by a canopy of trees but did not obstruct the Japanese gunners' view of the American position on the beach. To make matters worse, 3rd Battalion only had one working radio making communication and coordination between the two elements of the 162nd almost impossible. As the day wore on, it became clear that the advance toward Mokmer would be impossible unless the American forces could establish some control over the high ground. Since the 3rd Battalion could not accomplish this goal, the decision was made to withdraw the 3rd so it could rejoin the 2nd Battalion. This attempted move led to intensified attacks from the Japanese that prevented the 3rd from escaping. The lack of communication made it difficult for the 3rd Battalion to coordinate effective artillery fire as they beat back wave after wave of attacking Japanese soldiers. Compounding the problems of their precarious situation, the 3rd Battalion began to run low on ammunition and medical supplies. To resupply them landing craft brought down the coast made quick dashes to the beach under enemy fire, dropped off supplies, and evacuated the wounded. As the sun began to go down, four tanks from the 703rd Tank Company were brought forward to cover the 3rd Battalion's escape. Their presence, and a coordinated naval and artillery bombardment of the Japanese position, allowed the 3rd Battalion to retreat and rejoin the 2nd Battalion. Despite the ease with which the 186th had been accomplishing its objectives, the strength of the Japanese position and the casualties of the 162nd Regiment led Hurricane Task Force Commander General Horace Fuller to describe the situation on Biak after two days of fighting as "grave." He requested that the 163rd Regiment be brought out of reserve and brought to Biak to join the fight.

Day three of the Biak invasion saw the Japanese launch a counterattack on the 162nd's position that included tanks. When the American tanks moved up to engage them, the first fight between tanks during the Pacific War began. It was a one-sided affair. The Japanese tanks rushed forward in single file allowing the American tanks to concentrate their fire and destroy each tank in turn. The Japanese did not call off their attack when their tanks failed. In most places the 162nd repelled these attacks, but for a brief time the Japanese attack succeeded in once again dividing the 162nd. That attack was finally turned back by an artillery unit that picked up their rifles and fought as infantrymen. An estimated 400 Japanese soldiers had been killed, but casualties for the 162nd were also high.[5]

One of the Japanese tanks destroyed near the Parai Defile on Biak during one of the few tank battles of the war in the Pacific. (National Archives)

Two things became clear after these first three days of fighting on Biak. First, there were more Japanese soldiers on Biak than Allied planners had expected. Military Intelligence had figured on only six thousand enemy soldiers, when in reality there were twice that number.[6] Second, the Mokmer Airdrome could not be taken from the beach if the Japanese controlled the cliffs and bluffs overlooking it. The decision was made to withdraw the 162nd further toward Bosnek to re-establish contact with the 186th Regiment. This would allow them to coordinate their efforts and formulate a new plan of attack.[7]

The 1st and 3rd Battalions of the 163rd arrived at the landing area at Bosnek on June 1. They took over beachhead security and patrols in the area of Bosnek from the 186th. Different elements of the regiment helped secure one of the few sources of fresh water on Biak and began patrolling the beach and cliff area west of Bosnek. A 1st Battalion Company searched and secured two small islands off the coast of Biak that would be used as a firebase for the field artillery.[8]

Freed from shore patrol by the 163rd, the 186th moved north and inland, reducing a Japanese held position, and then maneuvered into position for a drive towards Mokmer from the interior behind the coastal cliffs and ridges. On June 2 the 186th fought off a Japanese counterattack and then began their move west. At the same time, the 162nd resumed their move west down the beach destroying Japanese defensive positions in the cliffs as they went. Both groups made slow, but real progress.[9]

On June 4, U.S. Intelligence received news of a Japanese flotilla made up of battleships, cruisers, destroyers, and troopships headed for Biak and moving fast. There was no surface fleet close enough to beat the Japanese to Biak, which left the Americans on the island worried about having to fight the Japanese in the cliffs on one side and on the beaches on the other. That, plus the prospect of a Japanese naval bombardment on their positions made clear how vulnerable the American foothold on Biak was. The Field Artillery aimed their guns out to sea in preparation for the appearance of the Japanese fleet forcing the units of the 41st Division to pause their attack. The men of the Hurricane Task Force had no way of knowing that several flights of B-25s and B-24s that had been dispatched to attack the Japanese fleet did enough damage to turn their ships back. When a U.S. surface fleet made up of cruisers and destroyers sped by on their way to intercept the Japanese, the Americans near the beach cheered them on.[10]

When able to resume their attacks the 186th made rapid progress across the interior plain of Biak while the 162nd had a much tougher fight. On June 7 both regiments converged on the Mokmer airstrip—the 186th from behind enemy positions on the high ground and elements of the 162nd from landing craft that transported them past the impassible stretches of the beach east of Mokmer. With solid support from field artillery units, they took the airstrip. Despite controlling the airstrip itself, the Americans had not driven the Japanese from all of their cliffside positions. From those positions enemy troops could direct mortar and machine-gun fire on American positions and coordinate infantry attacks. A Japanese attack on June 8 overran some American positions and the fight to re-establish their defensive security continued until the next day. This made the American position at Mokmer more secure, but the Japanese continued to bombard the area around the airstrip. It would take days to drive the Japanese from all their positions and until they were driven out, the airstrip at Mokmer was unusable for the American air force.[11]

In addition to the positions the Japanese held overlooking the Mokmer strip, they also still held strong defensive positions in the cliffs and ridges overlooking the beach between Mokmer and Bosnek. From these positions they could fire down on American units trying to use the beach as a path between the two American held positions. The Americans were unaware that the ridges above the road were peppered with caves some of which were connected to one another. The Japanese had converted many of these caves into bunkers. They had also constructed log pillboxes and bunkers in the ridges to guard the approaches to the caves. The 162nd split its activities between the cliff positions along the beach and those overlooking Mokmer. They successfully drove the Japanese from their position at the Parai Defile on June 12. At the same time other elements of the regiment began a series of attacks coordinated with the 186th on the Japanese defensive positions to the northwest of Mokmer.[12]

By June 15, the 162nd and 186th had been fighting a large, motivated, well-entrenched enemy for more than two weeks and the only other infantry unit on the island was the 163rd. General Fuller requested reinforcements. On June 18, the 34th Infantry and the 24th Infantry

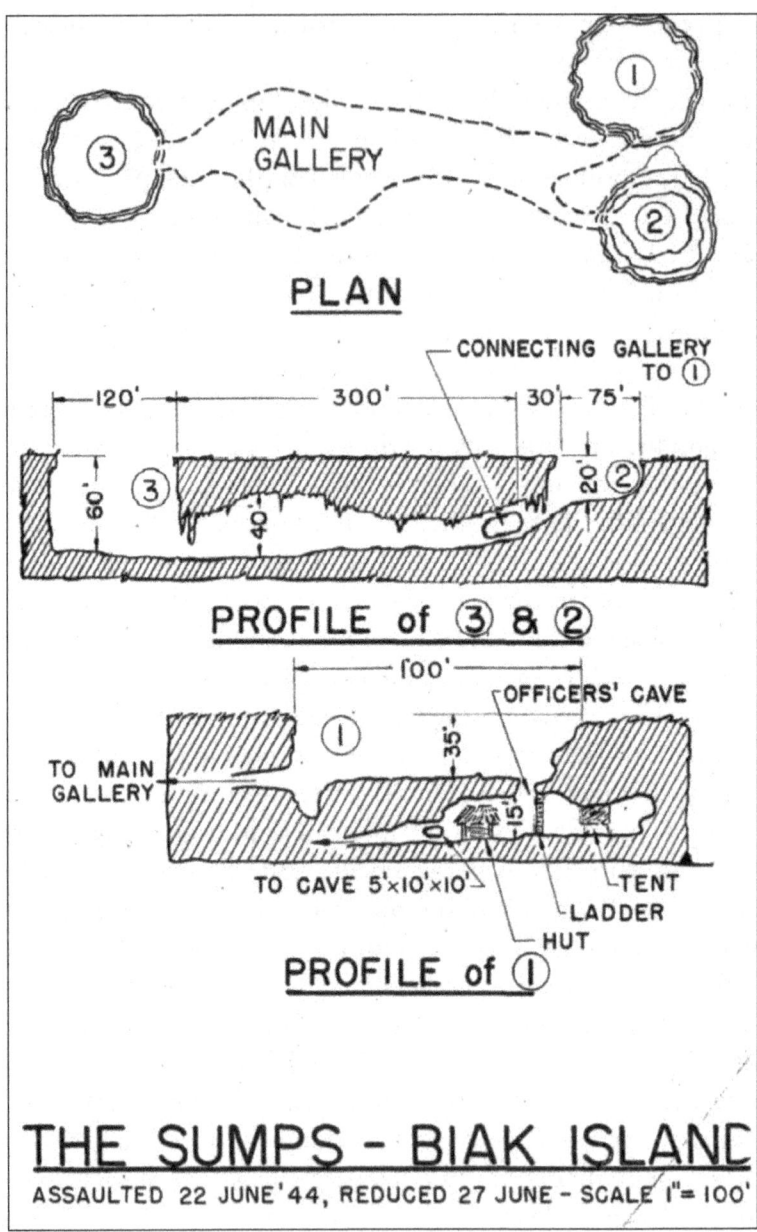

Diagram of "the Sumps" at Biak. The Japanese took advantage of a number of connected caves on Biak to create defensive positions that were very difficult for U.S. forces to overcome. Please note that the image is no longer to scale. (U.S. Army Center of Military History)

landed on the Biak near the Japanese Airdrome at Borokoe. They met only light resistance. But it was too late for General Fuller. His failure to quickly capture Mokmer and the other Japanese Airdromes cost him his job. He was removed from command of the Hurricane Task Force and replaced by one of MacArthur's favorite General Robert Eichelberger. It was General Eichelberger that MacArthur sent to New Guinea in 1942 to break through the Japanese at Buna and it was Eichelberger that MacArthur entrusted with the job of ending the fighting on Biak.[13]

With Eichelberger in charge and more men on the island the situation improved for the Americans on Biak. The 24th and the 34th Infantry operating to the west of Mokmer seized the airstrips at Borokoe and Sorido on June 20 and began moving east to support the operations of the 162nd and 186th. A coordinated series of attacks and patrols by the 162nd and 186th on the Japanese held high ground to the northwest of Mokmer culminated in a day's long struggle to destroy the Japanese occupying three, large, interconnected caves known as "the Sumps." The caves that made up "the Sumps" were not only connected to one another, each contained a series of galleries and antechambers in which the Japanese could shelter during bombings and bombardments, and which contained enough supplies for a large force to hold out for weeks. That was exactly what the Japanese had in mind. As was common in most places where the Japanese were trapped by the Allies, they refused to surrender intending to hold out for as long as possible. Artillery and conventional bombing had little effect even when they managed direct hits on the cave openings. Frustrated GIs simply poured gasoline through any fissure in the rocks above one of the caves and ignited it. The resulting fire set off explosions deep underground as the fire reached the stores of Japanese ammunition. The Americans hoped that most of the Japanese had been killed, but that night the Japanese attacked the American lines and were repulsed with heavy losses. The survivors of that attack returned to "the Sumps" and fought on. As American frustration grew, they came up with another plan to clear the main cave. They lowered an 850-pound charge of explosives into the cave and detonated it. This killed most of the remaining Japanese defenders of "the Sumps" and the area was finally cleared on June 27.[14]

With the airfields at Mokmer, Borokoe, and Sorido secured Eichelberger focused on eliminating the remaining pockets of Japanese resistance in the ridges near Ibdi that overlooked the beach between Mokmer and Bosnek. He assigned this job to the newly arrived 163rd Regiment.[15]

On June 11, the 2nd Battalion of the 163rd landed on Biak. They were the last major element of the 41st Division to arrive on the island and their landing near Bosnek was less than auspicious. Threats of a Japanese airstrike on the 2nd Battalion's landing sight delayed their landing by a day, but they hit the beach at Bosnek with no opposition and began taking up defensive positions occupied by other elements of the 163rd. No sooner had they moved into these positions than the antiaircraft on the destroyers offshore and on the beach opened fire on a group of Japanese planes. Two Japanese dive-bombers were hit and caught fire splashing down into the ocean, but one of their bombs hit the USS *Kalk* anchored near shore. As the third Japanese dive-bomber crashed into the ocean, the American ship caught fire and exploded. A heroic effort by the ship's crew prevented it from sinking. The men of the 2nd Battalion had to dive into whatever cover they could find as Japanese fighters strafed their positions on the beach. There were no casualties. Their chaotic arrival should have been an omen of what their weeks of fighting the Japanese in the caves and ridges of Biak would be like.[16]

After surviving the Japanese air raid on their landing area Company G and the rest of the 2nd Battalion received orders to deploy to an area between Bosnek and Mokmer. They were driven to the Ibdi area in trucks where they took up a position guarding the road along the beach. They were greeted by members of an antitank company that had just fought an engagement with the Japanese in the jungle covered coral ridges above the beach. They had lost a man and had been unable to recover his body. With that grim introduction the main body of Company G set up their base of operations in a coral valley that provided cover from enemy fire while two platoons climbed to positions in the coral ridges.[17]

Together with the 1st Battalion, 2nd Battalion began aggressive patrols designed to locate and destroy Japanese positions in the coral cliffs between Bosnek and Mokmer that had been bypassed during the drive for the Mokmer drome. The focus of their patrols was just north of the small coastal village of Ibdi. Meanwhile 3rd Battalion moved across Biak to play a role in the reduction of "the Sumps."[18]

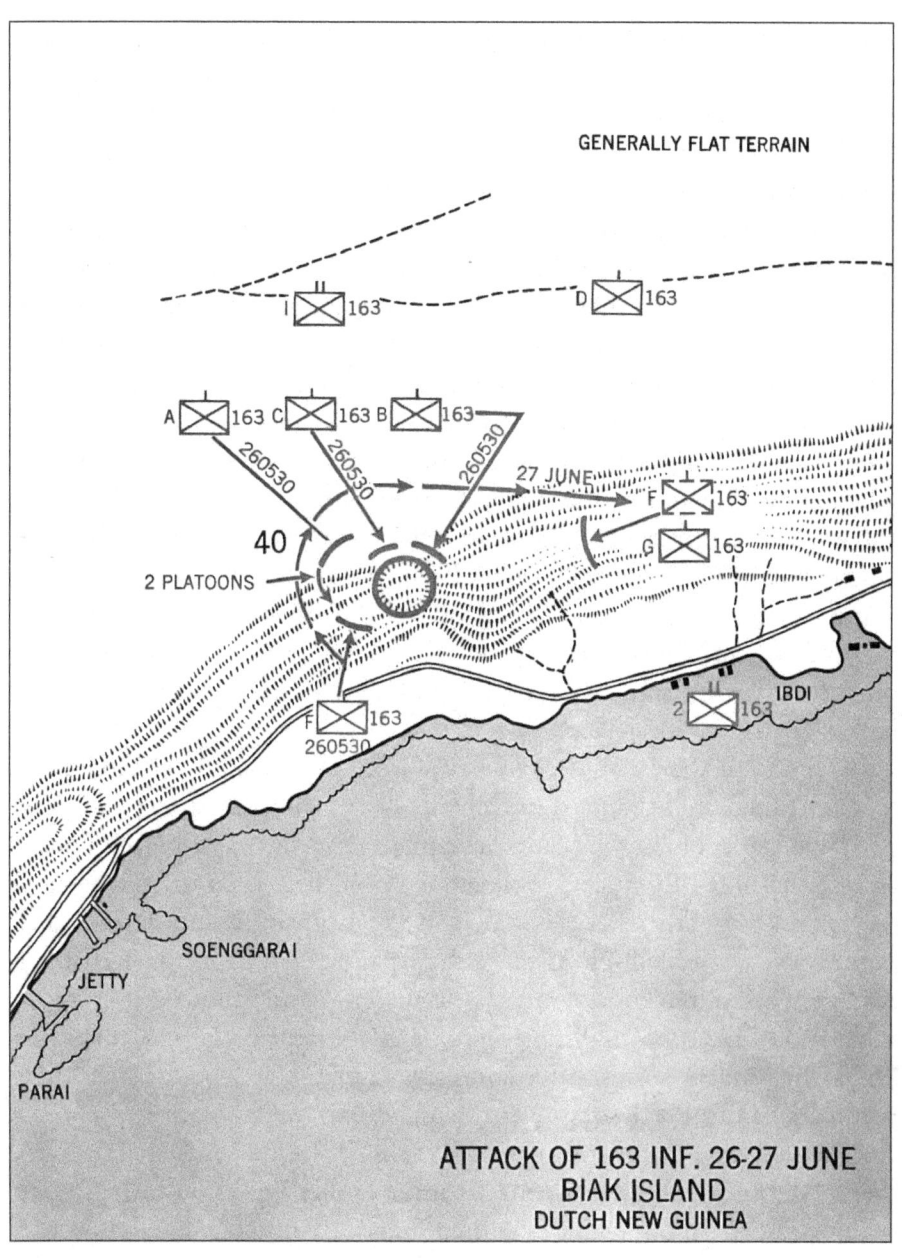

Map showing the location of Company G during the fighting around the Ibdi Pocket. (U.S. Army Center of Military History)

During Company G's time fighting in and around the Ibdi pocket they depended on a supply company to bring them water, food, and ammunition. Unusually in the strictly segregated U.S. Army of the 1940s, Company G's supply company at Biak consisted of Black soldiers, none of whom wore any insignia or sign of rank. They had been a quartermaster company assigned to a base in New Guinea and under the command of an absentee White captain and a violent racist first sergeant who verbally and physically abused them. When the first sergeant did not report for roll call one day and the captain asked where he was, one of the men made a remark indicating the condition in which he could be found. The sergeant was found hanging from a tree and an investigation into his murder began. All the Black men in the company swore not to talk and when none of them did, they were stripped of their company designation and rank and sent to the front to act as a combat supply company. These were the men who carried the heavy water tanks, boxes of ammunition, mortar shells, and food up the steep peaks surrounding the Ibdi Pocket. They did their job well. So well that Jack Anderson let one of the men man a lookout post with rifle in hand so that he could have a chance to shoot at the enemy.[19]

By June 15, the Japanese had figured out the location of Company G, 2nd Battalion headquarters, and its base camp. At sunset Japanese 75mms began lobbing shells into the American position. A shell exploded among the 116th Engineers. When a weapons platoon mortar answered the enemy fire, the Japanese zeroed in on its position and destroyed it as the crew scrambled for cover. If the Japanese had kept up a sustained barrage, committed more guns to the shelling, and followed it with an infantry attack, they might have crippled Company G and much of 2nd Battalion. As it was, one Company G man was wounded and five members of the 116th were wounded and two were killed.[20]

The next day, Company G patrols climbed the trails that led up into the coral ridges to search for the Japanese artillery guns with the intent of knocking them out and killing their crews. By June 17, it had become clear that the Japanese had moved further west and preparations for an attack on the Ibdi Pocket went into effect. Company F moved into position for the attack. Mortars from Company G's weapons platoon and Company H heavy mortars established a firebase on the beach.[21]

Given the depleted ranks of Company G, Jack Anderson, though only a sergeant, was put in charge of the company's 2nd Platoon and performed the work of an officer. This created memorable and often unpleasant duties for him during the fighting on Biak. On one occasion he had to deal with a soldier who refused to go on patrol. The soldier had separated himself from his squad and stood, rifle in hand, proclaiming that he was not going up into the ridges that day. When Anderson approached, the soldier leveled his rifle as though he intended to shoot. Anderson tried threats and then reason, but the man would not be persuaded. So, Anderson took a different approach. He turned as if to walk away and then spun around, charged at the soldier, wrestled him to the ground, and took his weapon away. After telling the soldier beneath him exactly what he thought about him, he let him up and ordered him to go on the patrol. The soldier retrieved his rifle and went. That soldier was killed a few days later and Anderson had the uncomfortable duty of writing a condolence letter to the family of a man for whom he had little respect. Another such letter proved even more difficult because it was for a friend killed during Company G's big assault on the Ibdi Pocket.[22]

As a member of Company G's weapons platoon, Bruce did not go up into the coral ridges before June 17. Initially the mortar section of the weapons platoon, of which Bruce was squad leader, established a firebase on the beach from which they could provide some artillery support for the company's rifle platoons.

On June 17, Sergeant Otis Belin, a good friend of Bruce's, came down from the ridges and asked Bruce if they could talk. They found a log washed up on the beach and sat down. Belin told him that if combat on the ridge continued as it had been he was sure that he would be killed. He left Bruce with instructions for who to contact and where to send his money and effects before returning to his platoon. Bruce was to write to his brother in Houston and direct his money to the widow of his older brother and their children.[23]

On June 18, Company F attacked the Japanese near Ibdi. They climbed up through the jungle that clung to the coral cliffs and followed a trail until they encountered a Japanese position. They met strong resistance that forced Company F back to a defensible position that it could hold in case the Japanese launched a counterattack. Following the failure of

Company F to dislodge the Japanese from Ibdi Pocket two Company G patrols made up of men from 2nd and 3rd Platoon received orders to patrol the area around the pocket to reconnoiter the Japanese position.

The trails the Americans followed went up steeply through the jungle and disappeared behind rocks and creeping trees. To the GIs, the landscape seemed filled with ambush points and they were convinced that a network of caves existed that allowed the Japanese to move around unseen so they could pop up in unexpected places. American soldiers learned to anticipate ambushes and to locate Japanese soldiers by smell from the mix of tobacco and their body odor. Still, ambushes happened often enough to make this a realistic fear.[24]

Twenty-eight men from 2nd Platoon led by First Lieutenant William Brandon and including Jack Anderson and Bruce's good friend Otis Belin set out to explore a trail that led up into the ridges where it met an east to west running track that a company patrol had reached the previous day. In a heavy morning rain, they covered hundreds of yards of trail passing abandoned Japanese positions and the bodies of dead Japanese soldiers. They strung a communications line along behind them so they could stay in contact with headquarters. They made it to the east–west track without incident.

They paused at the juncture of the trail and the track to call back to company command to let them know their location and what they had learned before moving west along the track. After hiking several hundred yards they discovered a firing lane that had been cut through the jungle to allow the Japanese to cover the track. At that point they tried to call in their position and location again and found that their radio link had stopped working. Two men were sent back to check the wire and found that it had been cut. They reconnected the wire, returned to the platoon and the patrol continued with a growing sense that the enemy was all around them.

They stopped at an intersection of another trail where six men were dispatched to search the southern part of the trail for signs of the enemy. They returned with reports of lots of evidence of the presence of the Japanese, but without seeing any enemy troops. When that group returned to the main body of the platoon a similarly sized group continued west along the track for several hundred yards again finding signs that the enemy was nearby but without encountering any Japanese soldiers. Lieutenant Brandon attempted to call in to Company Headquarters and found that the phone connection had stopped working for a second time. Convinced that they were surrounded, Anderson and the other platoon sergeants wanted to turn back but Lieutenant Brandon ordered the patrol to continue along the northern portion of the trail.

The steep and narrow trail forced the men of the patrol to move in single file as they climbed upwards. After a hundred yards the three-man scout group which included Sergeant Belin came to a small clearing that contained numerous small coral outcroppings and trees that had been cut down so they fell across the trail. A small ridge containing a significant number of openings overlooked the clearing. The scout group stopped to figure out their location and to discuss how to proceed. When they realized that they were where a Company F platoon had been attacked the day before they turned to leave. At that moment a Japanese sniper fired a shot. The round pierced one man's elbow and continued on, striking Belin in his midsection. Immediately a Japanese machine gun and other small arms fire poured down on the Company G men who took cover behind a log. Mortar rounds also begin to fall on the area. When the enemy fire let up the man shot in the elbow managed to bandage his wound but there was nothing that could be done for Belin. Anytime a member of the scout group tried to move, the Japanese opened fire. They were trapped where they lay. Lieutenant Brandon signaled for six men from the main body of the patrol to move forward to rescue the scouts. They rushed up the trail as the other members of the patrol shouted encouragement. Their attack caught the Japanese by surprise and bought enough time for the unwounded member of the scout group to escape and the wounded man to drag himself and Belin to safety.[25]

The men of 2nd Platoon then hurried back to company base having discovered that the Japanese were well dug in and present in significant numbers. This convinced battalion command that clearing the Ibdi Pocket would require a larger attack than that of Company F on the 18th. The patrol had been successful, but Otis Belin died of his stomach wound just as he had told Bruce he feared he would. When Doyle Bruce learned of his death he wept and spent most of the night of the 19th grieving.[26]

The second Company G patrol that set out on the 18th was made up mostly of men from the 3rd Platoon, among them Hargis Westerfield. The patrol left the company's beach base camp near Ibdi and climbed directly up into the ridges above. They passed through 1st Platoon which held an advanced position along the narrow trail. The covered body of a dead soldier from 1st Platoon lay along the trail waiting to be carried down. A little further on they passed the body of a Japanese soldier who had been shot and fallen from a cliff. His body had gotten caught in vines as he fell, and he hung suspended above the valley floor.

The trail they climbed ended at the base of a huge tree. The patrol's scouts indicated to the men that they would have to climb up and over the tree in groups of two. Hargis Westerfield was in the first pair. He and his partner climbed hand over hand using the trees exposed roots as handholds. On the other side of the tree they found a wide coral shelf overlooked by a low ridge ahead of them. Just as Westerfield and his partner took up positions on the shelf, Japanese mortars began firing on them. One of the shells bounced off a coral outcropping to their right and exploded. Several pieces of shrapnel buried themselves in Westerfield's shoulder, but his partner was blinded and more severely injured. Westerfield began to retreat from their position, but the other men of the patrol encouraged him to try to rescue the more severely injured man as mortar shells continued to fall around them. He managed to pull the man to the tree where he and other members of the patrol got him out of the direct line of fire. Westerfield and others covered the patrol's retreat down the trail before following back through 1st Platoon's position.

Eight members of the 3rd Platoon patrol were wounded, and one member of 1st Platoon's leg was severely broken when a member of the patrol who ran down the trail to escape enemy fire fell on him. The man that Westerfield helped to rescue died of his wounds several weeks later.[27] Evacuating even a single wounded man from the steep coral ridges of Biak involved dozens of men. Stretcher bearers had to hang on to any available hold along the trail and hand the litter, with the wounded man strapped to it, on to the next group of men. It was a painstaking, precarious process for both the bearers and the wounded man.[28]

Continued patrols by Company G and other companies of the 163rd and regular mortar and artillery fire kept the Japanese defenders of the Ibdi Pocket in constant danger as the Americans prepared for a full-scale attack. But another attack by Company F failed to destroy the Japanese position. On June 22, all of Company G's platoons took up positions in the ridges east of the Ibdi Pocket and battled the Japanese dug in on those ridges during the daylight hours for the next two days. On the night of June 24, the beleaguered men of Company G made their way back down the steep trails to the beach.[29]

After Company F's initial contact with the Japanese position at Ibdi the American artillery kept up a steady, but in the end ineffective, barrage against the enemy sheltered in the caves. On June 24, B-25s bombed Ibdi Pocket with little effect, but they were able to survey the Japanese position. From the air it was clear that the main Japanese defensive position was a large hole in the cliffs that probably, based on what the Americans had learned at "the Sumps," connected to a network of other smaller caves. To eliminate these positions, division command planned a coordinated attack involving elements of the 163rd's 1st and 2nd Battalions. On June 26, Companies F and G began an attack in the early morning hours that made significant progress.[30]

Company G returned to the ridges to mount another attack on the Ibdi Pocket the following day. Two Company G patrols ran into heavy enemy fire. The 3rd Platoon advance was stopped again near the location where they had been turned back the week before. They lost one man and several others were wounded. North of their position, Company G's larger force moved through many abandoned Japanese defensive positions before running into a pillbox containing a heavy machine gun that cut down their lead scout before its crew was driven from the position. Continuing its advance up and over the ridge, they covered fifty yards and secured the ridge that had stopped their progress for days only to face a still taller ridge in front of them. They tried an enveloping maneuver against the Japanese position on that ridge but were stopped again by machine-gun fire that killed another of Company G's men before the advance reached a place of safety. Japanese knee mortars launched from the ridge began landing among the Americans, killing two more and wounding another.[31]

When the company moved back into the ridges after the bombardment on June 24, its strength was far below optimal levels. Since mortars had proven ineffective at reducing Japanese defenses on the ridges, Doyle Bruce and the other men of the mortar squad were folded into a rifle platoon and went up the steep trails in preparation for the attack on the Ibdi Pocket on June 26.

Like the other men who spent time on these ridges, Bruce recalled the steepness of the trails. According to him men had to hold onto tree trunks to keep from sliding down when they came to a halt. During a firefight, Bruce took cover behind a tree that became the focus of enemy fire. He felt that a Japanese soldier watched that tree for any sign of movement so he could shoot and kill him. Covering fire from the rest of the company eventually allowed Bruce and others to safely withdraw.[32]

Bruce Baird had missed much of the fighting around the Ibdi Pocket due to illness, but on June 27, he ascended the ridges with his platoon and advanced in support of another attack by Company F on the left. The advance continued until a company scout reported the location of a dirt and log dugout big enough to hold three men on the trail ahead and another similar structure higher up on the ridges. Baird stationed a man with a rifle with a scope in a protected position from which he could fire on the opening of the first dugout. He then led two men forward, one whose rifle had a grenade launcher attachment forward in an attempt to take out any Japanese soldiers in the dugout. Baird and his men took cover behind a chest-high coral shelf and approached to a distance within the range of the grenade launcher. His plan was for all three men to pop up and fire on the dugout opening in the hope that the grenade launcher would be accurate. When they popped up a single Japanese rifle fired. One of the two men with Baird dropped to the ground so fast he badly hurt his knee and could not walk. Baird himself dove below the coral shelf and was unhurt. The man with the grenade launcher had been killed by a Japanese sniper. Under covering fire from the soldier with the scope Baird picked the injured man up on his back and made it to safety. Baird's platoon made no more progress that day.[33]

The next day both companies again resumed their attacks with little effect. At the end of that day's fighting, only forty-two men of Company F and only sixty-five men of Company G were fit for action. Battalion

Combat engineers at a cave entrance possibly being used by the Japanese in 1944. Dynamite was often used to collapse small caves. (National Archives)

command called off their attacks on the Ibdi Pocket and resorted to shelling the Japanese position almost constantly.[34]

Company G remained in a holding position on the ridges, losing another man to rifle fire and another man wounded, before being pulled off the front lines on July 4 and driven to a safe location down the beach. There they were able to bathe and wash their clothes for the first time in weeks. Ten men from Company G had been killed in the ridges near the Ibdi Pocket and dozens more were wounded during the more than two weeks of continuous fighting. They had fought the Japanese on the steep ridges, in manmade pillboxes and trenches, and in naturally occurring caves large and small. Enemy rifles, light and heavy machine guns, knee mortars and heavy artillery had all taken their toll. The combat at Ibdi Pocket left physical and mental scars on the Company G survivors which many would remember as their worst combat experience.[35]

While 1st and 2nd Battalions fought to clear the Ibdi Pocket, the 163rd Regiment's 3rd Battalion participated in the reduction of a position known as the East Caves which, though lightly defended, the Japanese used to create chaos. That position was cleared with the help of a flight of P-40s on July 4, 1944.[36]

Following a brief period of rest during which they broke in replacements sent to fill in the large gaps in their ranks, the men of Company G moved from regimental command onto the plains behind the ridges to carry out mopping up patrols designed to kill Japanese soldiers fleeing the constant bombardment of Ibdi Pocket.

Hargis Westerfield had been in the thick of the fighting at Ibdi Pocket and had not come through the experience unscathed. Like the other men of Company G his time at headquarters after the fight for the pocket provided him with sleep, food, and rest in abundance. That came to an end on July 18 when the company received orders to move inland and patrol west along the flat scrub land behind the coral ridges where they had been fighting.[37]

As an experienced member of Company G, Westerfield took on added responsibilities. On the company's second day out, his platoon sergeant assigned him the role of lead scout. The sergeant assured him the job would be easy because the company had been joined by a scout dog trained to detect the presence of enemy soldiers. The dog came with a sergeant who followed it holding a leash. Westerfield disliked patrolling with the dog because when the shooting started, the dog and its handler would escape to the rear under covering fire from the men of the company. As lead scout it was his job to protect the dog at all costs. Learning that his safety came second to the safety of a dog did not endear the dog to Westerfield. The patrol that he led encountered no Japanese soldiers, but the soldier who took over the role of lead scout duties from Westerfield walked right up on a Japanese soldier and killed him. The dog had not detected the enemy soldier.[38] The scout dogs had made their first appearance among the men of Company G during the fight for Ibdi Pocket. Jack Anderson's platoon had been given one for one of their patrols and he was not impressed. Like Westerfeld, Anderson quickly developed a dislike of the scout dogs. One of the times that one of the dogs worked with his platoon and signaled the presence of Japanese soldiers, the dog and its handler got in the way and prevented his men from engaging the enemy directly while putting the platoon at risk. On another occasion the platoon's human scout saw the enemy before the dog detected them.[39] Even Baird, who usually took a positive view of things, felt that the scout dogs might cause more problems for the men than they would prove to be worth.[40]

The inland patrols continued until July 21st when Company G connected its position to those of the 186th. At that point, some platoons were selected to establish ambushes along the trails leading out of the Ibdi Pocket. Their mission involved lying in wait along the trails and roads leading away from it from which they could surprise and kill escaping Japanese soldiers and prevent them from rejoining other Japanese units scattered across Biak. Along with units from the 186th to their west, they created a killing zone that proved difficult for the Japanese to escape. These patrols and ambushes gave the replacement soldiers who had joined the company after July 4 a taste of combat at a minimal risk.

A guide dog working with a U.S. soldier on Biak 1944. (National Archives)

Westerfield's 3rd Platoon was one of those chosen for ambush duty. From his ambush point he witnessed the heavy bombing of the doomed Japanese garrison that had fought the 163rd for six weeks. Japanese escapees walked into the 3rd Platoon ambush a few times over the following week. The first encounter with the enemy did not go well. Three Japanese soldiers escaped when one of the men in Westerfield's group opened fire too soon. The next day Westerfield and another soldier had taken over the platoon's advance position. They did not expect to see any Japanese because they were sure that the failure of the day before had alerted the enemy to their position. When they heard movement on the trail behind them, they assumed it was men from their own platoon bringing up their rations for the day. Instead, a lone Japanese soldier emerged from the undergrowth. Westerfield took aim and shot the man. He was the first enemy soldier that Westerfield killed. That same afternoon a small group of enemy soldiers came out of the jungle near the platoon's base camp, surprising the GIs who killed them all.

Similar encounters continued for the rest of the week that Westerfield and 3rd Platoon spent in ambush. Though the platoon killed many who attempted to cross their area, Westerfield did not see any more Japanese soldiers. The platoon was relieved on July 28 and returned to regimental base camp in trucks. From there they boarded LCTs and were transferred to the Korim Bay area of Biak to recuperate and carry out light patrolling duties.[41]

At this camp the army had put up large tents for barracks and neatly arranged everything along strait roads that made it easy for the men to find their way around. Several kitchens had been built so the men in camp were well fed. In their free time some of the men tried to come up with ways to make alcohol without a still, a process Bruce Baird feared would result in their poisoning. While living in camp Baird's health again failed him. He developed a sore on his foot that prevented him from participating in company patrols around the area. Health problems were common among Company G veterans, and most were in and out of the hospital. Few of them reported for duty every day while in camp. Just as Baird's foot began to heal and he was able to resume his duties he contracted hepatitis. This required a transfer via landing craft to a hospital facility located away from camp on the beach. Here Baird received word that he had earned enough points for transfer back to the United States. In August he and a few dozen other Company G men eligible for rotation traveled to Finschhafen where they waited for enough men to make a shipload. They sailed for the United States on board an older ship from the Netherlands that Baird remembered as serving excellent food. The only problem on the way home was that a dock workers strike in San Fransisco diverted their ship to Seattle. Baird arrived back at Fort Lewis in November of 1944. Though it took some time to get seats on a train, Baird was home in Ogden, Utah by Thanksgiving evening.[42]

On August 15, Jack Anderson's commission as a second lieutenant came through. He was sworn in by his company commander Buck Braman with a set of borrowed second lieutenant's bars. Anderson's new assignment sent him to join Company G of the 186th Regiment. His combat tour would continue, but he would no longer be a member of MacArthur's Bloody Butchers.[43]

CHAPTER 10

The Philippines

February 27, 1945–April 1, 1945

By marshalling his land, naval, and air resources to land his men in unexpected places behind areas of Japanese troop concentrations where they secured airfields he could use to cover his next bold move, General Douglas MacArthur wrong footed Japanese military leaders and achieved stunning and rapid success. U.S. landings at New Britain, Salamaua, Finschhafen, Hollandia, Aitape, and Wakde had gained territory in big leaps while keeping American casualties low. Each leap brought MacArthur closer to the Philippines. MacArthur's only mistake had been at Biak where he underestimated the problems presented by terrain and enemy troop strength. Despite this mistake by 1945 MacArthur's forces were poised to invade the Philippines.

The entire 41st Infantry Division spent eight months consolidating the American hold on Biak following the unexpected costly fight for control of the island. The various elements of the division had suffered casualties greater than in any fight since their battles for control of Buna–Sanananda–Gona and Salamaua in 1943. The time spent on Biak after the island was secured provided time for rest, recuperation, and replacements. While the 41st recovered, the war in the Pacific moved on without them. The navy and the Marines drove the Japanese from the Marianas and Guam, and U.S. air bases were constructed ever closer to the Japanese mainland. By the time the 41st was again fit for duty, General MacArthur's plans for invading the Philippines were already underway and American forces were dealing the Japanese devastating losses on land and at sea.

MacArthur began the invasion of the Philippines by landing elements of the 6th Army group on the island of Leyte. Because the Japanese had anticipated the American attack beginning on the large southernmost Philippine island of Mindanao, the American landing at Leyte threw their military forces on the islands into an immediate crisis. Japanese command rushed their navy into the waters near Leyte where they met a massive U.S. naval force that destroyed a significant amount of the remaining Japanese surface fleet. This gave the U.S. control of the waters around the Philippines. MacArthur took advantage of American naval superiority by landing another U.S. force on the island of Mindoro on December 12, 1944. Mindoro's location directly south of the Manilla Harbor led to the American landing on Luzon just a few days later.[1]

Near the end of January, the 41st Division began to leave Biak and reassemble on the island of Mindoro with the assumption that they would be a part of the invasion of Luzon. Instead, the 41st played a lead role in the liberation of the southern Philippines. By February 9, the entire division had assembled at the staging area on Mindoro. As had often been the case, the three infantry regiments that made up the core of the 41st Division were split up and went into combat in the Philippines at different times and in different places.[2]

After receiving his promotion Jack Anderson spent the remainder of his time on Biak getting to know the men of the platoon he commanded and learning the ropes of being an officer. During the division's time recuperating at Korim Bay, Anderson took advantage of a chance to take thirty days of R&R in Australia. As soon as allowed, he began to make his way to Gladstone where he expected to stay with the Connellans in a spare room. But when he arrived the room had been taken. The solution to his temporary homelessness was to move into the flat immediately below Dorothy's. He worried that this would raise eyebrows in the small community, but when Dorothy and her mother made it clear that would be fine, he moved in. He looked forward to spending a great deal of time with Dorothy. Unfortunately, he had a severe relapse of malaria during his first week in Gladstone. When he recovered Dorothy announced that she was taking time off and that they were going to Brisbane with the Connellans. They spent two weeks in the city and traveling around Australia. On the last night before Anderson boarded ship for the Philippines Dorothy took him aside and told him that it was the last time they would see one another. Anderson protested, but she insisted. She said they would continue to write one another until one of them got married and then they would stop.[3]

Shortly after returning from this break, Anderson and the men of the 186th made the move to Mindoro in the Philippines. Though not as luxurious as the base at Finschhafen, Anderson's brief stay provided him with some memorable opportunities. He and some other men helped a group of locals catch a sea turtle on the beach. They then butchered the turtle and cooked it. Anderson enjoyed the turtle steak, but decided the turtle eggs were not for him. On another occasion he and a group of GIs were relaxing on a beach when they noticed another soldier struggling to stay afloat in the strong tides just offshore. They swam out to help, but they could do little other than keep him from drowning while waiting for a small shore patrol vessel to rescue them all. Much of his time at Mindoro was taken up by administrative tasks like censoring the letters from members of his platoon and disciplining those who got out of line.[4]

The 186th Regiment was the first unit of the 41st Division to be sent into action in the Philippines. On February 28, the 186th landed on the island of Palawan. Their landings targeted the harbor at Puerto Princessa.[5] As a part of 2nd Battalion, Anderson and his platoon followed the 3rd Platoon onto the beaches at Palawan. They found few Japanese soldiers as they moved into Puerto Princesa. Anderson noted the novelty of being in a combat situation in an actual city with paved streets, running water, and electricity.[6] The 186th achieved all its first day objectives as the Japanese abandoned their coastal defenses to move to the island's interior highlands and jungles. This became a pattern the Japanese military followed at numerous locations throughout the battle for the Philippines. The 186th met no real resistance until March 2 as they approached the foothills and the Japanese inland defenses. A few days of coordinated attacks involving airstrikes and reinforced infantry attacks drove the Japanese from their defenses and secured control of Puerto Princessa.[7] Anderson and his men experienced almost no difficulty until they encountered a large group of Japanese soldiers dug in on a hill who were determined to fight, but the ability of allied bombers to drop bombs on their position meant their resistance was short lived. The 186th followed the Palawan landing with landings on the island chain that separated Palawan from Borneo and attacks on specific Japanese positions in the jungle where they were aided by Filipino rebels.[8] Most of Anderson's time on Palawan was spent in these small combat missions and in patrolling the island. He and his men were assisted by local Filipinos that he referred to as "Borobos." They were all former convicts from a prison on Palawan who escaped and engaged in a guerilla war against their Japanese occupiers. Anderson did not think much of their combat skills, but they were fierce fighters and excellent guides.[9]

It was also on Palawan that elements of the 41st first encountered evidence of Japanese cruelty to American prisoners of war. As men of the 186th closed in on their position, the Japanese soldiers in charge of a small POW camp crammed their American captives into an air-raid shelter, soaked the shelter in gasoline, and set it on fire. Any GI who escaped the inferno was cut down by Japanese machine-gun fire. Four Americans managed to escape by crawling through a tunnel that opened on a cliff face overlooking a stretch of beach. The men dropped from the tunnel to the sand many feet below. One of the GIs was hurt and later died from his injuries. The survivors' story no doubt increased the hatred that the men of the 41st felt for their Japanese enemies and made an ugly war even uglier.[10]

While the 186th Regiment made its landing on Palawan and proceeded to destroy the Japanese on that island, the two other regiments of the 41st Division prepared for their own Philippine landing. On March 8, the 162nd and 163rd Regiments left their camp on Mindoro and boarded troop transports headed south.[11] For three days the men of Company G traveled south from Mindoro across the Sulu Sea and lay off the coast of the Zamboanga Peninsula on the island of Mindanao on the morning of March 10.[12] They watched from the decks of their troop transports as guns from the U.S. Navy's cruisers and destroyers assigned to guard their passage south, along with bombs dropped by American bombers, lit up the beach where they were to land.[13]

Bombardment by the U.S. Navy and bombing by U.S. airplanes of the landing area had been underway since the ninth and continued to within a few minutes of the first waves of men from the 162nd Regiment hitting the beach of San Mateo just a few miles from Zamboanga City. That bombardment had driven the Japanese from their coastal defensives which meant that the initial landings were largely unopposed. As had become standard practice, the 162nd landed first and secured the beach, followed by the 163rd which moved through their position and began offensive operations. The plan was for the 163rd to land and then move

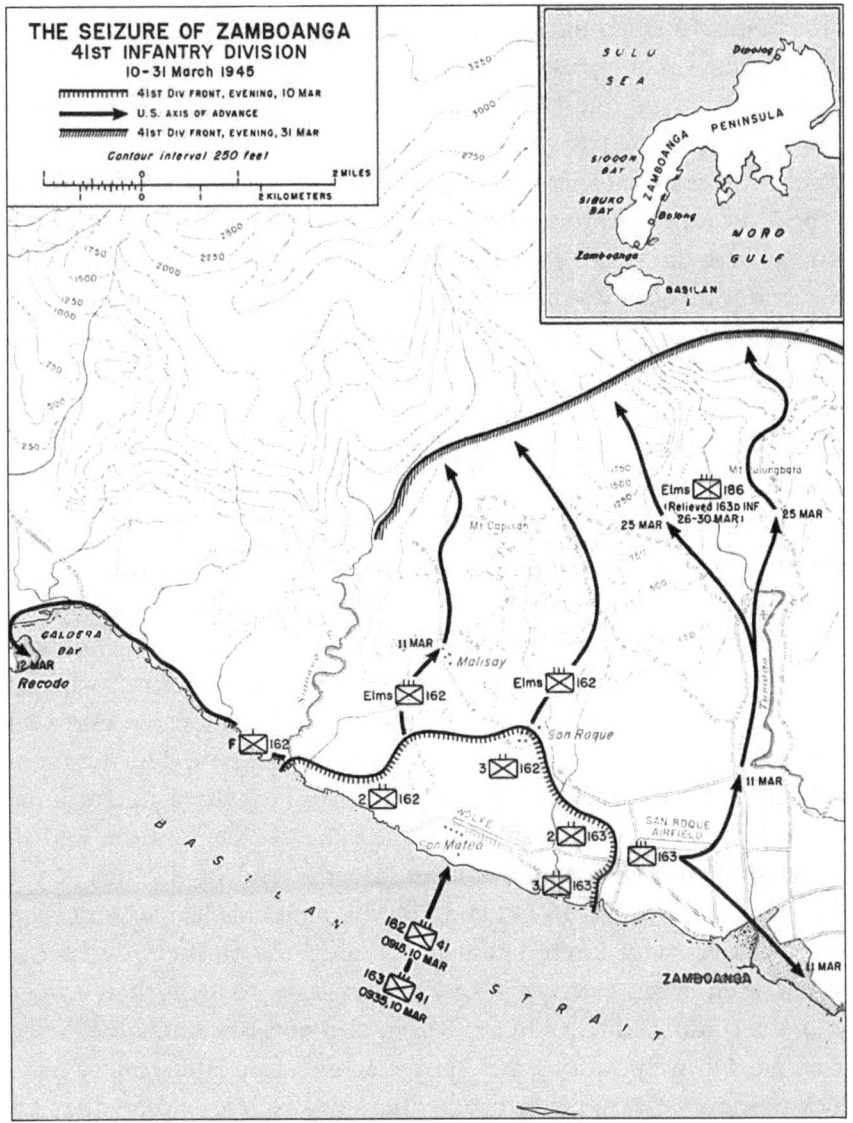

Map showing the path of the 163rd's invasion of Mindanao on the Zamboanga Pennisula in March 1945. (U.S. Army Center of Military History)

East toward Zamboanga City while the 162nd moved north into the foothills and jungles overlooking the beach.[14] As successive waves of landing craft carrying the men of the 163rd to the beach arrived, Japanese artillery and mortars located in the hills to the north began to rain shells onto the American beachhead. During the bombardment, a major was hit by shrapnel and a rookie soldier who ran out to help him was killed.[15]

From their landing craft the men of Company G watched the waves of transports carry the 162nd Regiment to the beach and surveyed the terrain where they would be fighting. As their transports sped toward the beach, Japanese mortar and artillery shells began to fall on the beachhead. A malfunctioning ramp forced the men of Company G to go over the side of the transport.[16] The seas on the approach to the beachhead near Zamboanga must have been exceptionally rough because all of the accounts of the landing mention terrible sea sickness. Doyle Bruce recalled that a bell mounted on the back of the boat to indicate when the boat was rolling too much in heavy seas rang the entire time, but there was nothing that could be done other than to get to the beach as fast as possible. By the time he landed, he was so nauseated that he felt that being hit by one of the Japanese mortar shells that had begun to fall around them might be a relief.[17]

After some minutes spent arranging all the companies into the proper position for advance, they moved east towards Zamboanga City. During the assault on Zamboanga, the 163rd attacked in battalion formation for the first time during the war with all three battalions arranged and advancing in a unified front as the regiment moved East. The regiment's 1st Battalion took up a position farthest north near the fringe of jungle and foothills, the 2nd Battalion occupied the center position, and the 3rd Battalion moved along the coast. By the end of the first day of fighting, all units of the 162nd and 163rd Regiments had accomplished their objectives with limited casualties due to the Japanese decision to abandon their beach defenses in order to continue to focus their artillery fire on the landing zone.[18] On the beach, elements of Company G seized Japanese defensive positions including machine guns and artillery pieces which demo teams later destroyed. The few Japanese soldiers they saw they killed, and the company reached the Basiliwan River by the end of the first day of fighting.[19]

On day two of the American attack, the 2nd Battalion crossed the Basiliwan River. When the 3rd Battalion broke through a stubborn pocket of Japanese soldiers defending the beach that same day the last real obstacle between the 163rd and Zamboanga City was eliminated. The biggest threat to the men of the 163rd as they closed in on the city were mines and booby traps the Japanese had left behind as they retreated. For a second straight day, Japanese artillery concentrated on the American beachhead at San Mateo, scoring a hit on a fuel depot at an airfield U.S. troops captured the previous day. The resulting fire sent a column of smoke into the air that was visible for miles, but naval guns were able to silence the Japanese artillery a short time later. The 3rd Battalion and Company G of 2nd Battalion spent the rest of the second day trying to clear pockets of Japanese defenders from Zamboanga City. The rest of the 2nd Battalion turned north in an attempt to capture the strategically important San Roque airdrome. Intense artillery fire and stiff resistance prevented 1st Battalion from capturing the airfield on the second day.[20] Company G spent part of that day supporting Company F's seizure of Santa Maria before being attached to the 3rd Battalion to help clear Zamboanga City of Japanese soldiers. This was the first and only time that Company G fought in an urban setting. Despite this lack of experience, the company fought effectively. Most of their action in Zamboanga City involved trying to clear a stone building of a large number of Japanese defenders. When tanks and artillery proved ineffective at driving them out, the men of 2nd Platoon threw flashbang grenades through the first story windows and rushed in and up to the second story where the stunned and wounded Japanese surrendered. In all Company G captured fifty-five enemy soldiers including three officers.[21]

On the third day, the combined effort of the 1st and 2nd Battalions led to the quick capture of San Roque while the 3rd Battalion finished clearing Zamboanga City. With these objectives met, the 163rd turned its attention to planning an assault on the Japanese defenses on the jungle covered high ground behind San Roque and in the Pasonanca Valley. The 1st and 2nd Battalions moved forward on either side of a highway that ran from Zamboanga City through the valley. Despite mines, booby traps, mortars, machine guns and field artillery, the 163rd made decent progress before the end of the third day. Meanwhile to their west, the 162nd Regiment began pushing into the high ground to the west of San Roque village but were driven back by intense artillery fire. With the airstrips near the beachhead at San Mateo up and running and the strip at San Roque already under repairs, both the 162nd and 163rd Regiments were able to count on small scout planes to help coordinate artillery cover by spotting and calling in the location of enemy emplacements. Despite the Americans progress and growing advantages, the Japanese remained in their defensive positions throughout the third day and appeared to be ready to defend them at all costs.[22] On March 12, the 1st and 2nd Battalion continued their move toward Pasonanca still following the highway with 2nd on the left side and the 1st on the right. They hoped that a rapid advance through the valley would allow them to bypass and isolate Japanese hilltop positions north of San Roque.[23] The road through the valley was mined and the Battalion encountered heavy machine gun and mortar fire as it advanced. The 2nd Battalion managed to gain 400 yards of ground before being stopped by a well-prepared series of Japanese defenses made up of trenches, pillboxes, log bunkers, and barbed wire.[24]

The assault on those positions began the next day. The Japanese had years to build up their defenses in and around Zamboanga and they had not wasted their time. To overcome the Japanese, the men of the 2nd Battalion had to survive machine-gun fire, mortars, trip wires and booby traps, as well has the heaviest and most sustained artillery fire they had ever faced.[25] Company G's third day at Zamboanga proved to be a terrifying one. They moved through Santa Maria village that had been captured the day before and headed for the carefully prepared and deep Japanese defenses. As the Company moved through a stand of coconut trees outside the town, mortar and artillery fire rained down blowing the tops out of the trees and wounding a number of the men of Company G.[26] To avoid the heavy fire, Company G maneuvered to a safer route of approach and attacked the Japanese position on its flank using all the skill of an experienced combat unit and all the resources at its disposal. Company command called in spotter planes to direct artillery fire, used its own mortar platoon to weaken entrenched enemy positions, and called up tanks to take out Japanese pillboxes.[27] Despite the wounded and the heavy enemy fire the company advanced several hundred yards

A Sherman tank equipped with a bulldozer blade advances into the hills near Zamboanga, accompanying men of the 163rd Infantry, March 1945. (National Archives)

to a crossroads where they were able to dig defensive positions in a gully that offered them some protection. In this defensive position, the men got a temporary break from enemy artillery and mortar fire, and took the chance to eat lunch.[28] Thanks to the scout plane flying overhead the 146th Field Artillery knocked out two of the heavy guns while Company G mortars lobbed shells into the Japanese trenches ahead of them.[29] The company renewed their attack and advanced across a rise of 400 yards and moved into the border of another grove of coconut trees. They were stopped after a few yards by intense machine-gun fire from Japanese pillboxes. Tanks rushed forward and took out the pillboxes, but Company G dug in where they were for the night.[30]

For Doyle Bruce, the attacks on the Japanese defenses during the ten days between March 13 and March 23 provided a number of unique and sometimes terrifying experiences. Japanese 75mm guns fired down on Company G as it advanced on March 13, subjecting Bruce and the

Men of the 163rd advance through a grove of coconut trees in the hills overlooking Zamboanga City and the San Roque Airdrome, March 1945. (National Archives)

others to their first experience of attacking while under real enemy artillery fire. The experience would become a common one. The fighting at Zamboanga also gave Bruce the chance, as leader of the company's mortar squad, to coordinate mortar fire efficiently and effectively on enemy positions. Many company attacks were preceded by mortar fire and on more than one occasion Bruce and his men were called on to knock out specific enemy gun emplacements or to reduce enemy trenches. In addition, Bruce and his men fired smoke grenades at enemy positions so that scout planes could call in accurate field artillery fire.[31]

Their defenses, carefully prepared over the weeks and months during which the Japanese believed the U.S. invasion of the Philippines would begin at Mindanao, consisted of rolls of razor wire, trenches, and log pillboxes. The Japanese had also prepared another deadly surprise for the Americans. Into the side of one hill, the Japanese had dug a deep mine and stuffed it with all kinds of explosives. On March 13, 2nd Battalion approached that hill. With Companies E and F in the lead and Company G in a trailing position, they fought their way through the Japanese defensive positions at the base of the hill and Company E began to ascend the slope. As they climbed, the men of Company E became scattered across the hill so that some men made the relatively flat top while others were still working their way up. Officers ordered a halt to their advance so that Company E could regroup before going forward. The company veterans at the top sat down to smoke and take a break. Just as Company G, following in reserve, reached the base of the hill, the Japanese detonated the mine deep inside the hill. The explosion was visible for miles around and, to the men of the 2nd Battalion, it appeared that the whole top of the hill had been blown into the air taking men, trees, and huge chunks of earth skyward. Casualties from the explosion and from the debris that rained down on the men of 1st and 2nd Battalions were high and included one man who was crushed by a falling tree. Debris from the explosion rose higher in the air than the observation plane flying above the battlefield directing field artillery fire. The explosion created a crater 300 yards wide in the top of the hill. Fortunately, much of the force of the explosion blew up the side of the hill opposite the side where the men of Company E had been advancing.[32]

On March 13, Company G moved forward in support of the advance made by Companies E and F. As Company E crested a small hill, the men of Company G were still among the tanks several yards behind. As they passed through the tanks, the top of the hill exploded in a rush of red flames and dirt that threw men, rocks, and trees high into the air. The debris fell just short of Company G's position which meant, unlike many of the other 1st and 2nd Battalion Companies, G escaped the detonation of "Blow-up Hill" unscathed. Casualties from the explosion were obviously highest among the men of Company E, but four companies from the 1st Battalion also suffered casualties from falling debris. Company B had one man killed. Company C sustained fourteen total casualties, Company A had four, and Company D had four. Company E had three men killed and eighteen wounded.[33] Estimated casualties across all units involved ran to eighty-three.

After recovering from the shock of the blast Company G moved forward in anticipation of a Japanese counterattack. When none came, a five-man patrol from G was sent forward to scout the far side of Blow-up Hill. As the patrol moved forward, Japanese artillery and mortars once again began to bombard Company G's position, wounding two men. When the barrage lifted, four members of the patrol scrambled back to rejoin the company. Mortar and machine-gun fire killed one man and wounded three of the others. Company commander Captain Braman ordered three men and two medics to go and retrieve the body of the man who had been killed. Despite walking into an area that they knew the Japanese had covered with machine guns and mortars, the recovery patrol recovered the body without incident.[34] The catastrophe that the men came to call Blow-up Hill did not stop the advance by the 1st and 2nd Battalions. Both groups continued to make progress seizing control of two geographically strategic points respectively before the end of the day.[35]

With both the 1st and 2nd Battalions in position, the push to gain control of the Pasonanca Valley began again on March 14, 1945. Coordinating their attacks with tank units and moving behind a screen of artillery and mortar fire, the 2nd Battalion advanced to a position just south of the town of Pasonanca. There stiff resistance and tough conditions made further progress unlikely without an attack on Japanese held high ground outside the town. That attack involved all the Battalions of the 162nd Infantry Regiment which had been operating to the west of the 163rd. The 162nd drove the Japanese from their position and the 163rd renewed their attack on the following day.[36]

The 1st and 2nd Battalion attacks of the 14th advanced under the umbrella of mortar and artillery fire which helped them capture several hundred yards of Japanese held territory. To the west the 162nd also made progress but were halted by a massive Japanese counterattack. At night, the Japanese attempted to infiltrate the perimeter established by the advanced companies of both regiments, making every night a time of potential danger for the GIs.[37] On March 14, Company G received orders to move forward into the valley behind Blow-up Hill and advance on the town of Pasonanca. The men nicknamed this area "Death Valley." An artillery barrage supported by Company mortars and flights of fighter bombers preceded the company's move forward,

Soldiers of the 163rd's 2nd Battalion pause their advance to allow a Sherman tank to move forward to eliminate Japanese defenses in the area around Pasonanca near Zamboanga, March 1945. (National Archives)

allowing them to advance hundreds of yards to a dense patch of jungle from which they could observe the rest of the valley through which they were advancing. A Company G scout counted eleven enemy pillboxes covering the road and even slight movement by the company's advance groups drew intense Japanese rifle, machine-gun, and mortar fire. As had become standard procedure, tanks were brought forward to deal with the obstacle. In desperation Japanese defenders focused their fire on the two Shermans that rumbled up the road, but the tanks systematically destroyed all eleven enemy pillboxes and took out an artillery emplacement for good measure.[38] Company G then followed the tanks and Company F forward to another road junction at the cost of two men wounded.[39]

The attacks of both the 162nd and the 163rd on March 15 were not only coordinated with each other, but also with tank companies, the air force, whose heavy bombers destroyed Japanese defenses and inflicted heavy casualties, as well as with field artillery which reduced

Japanese machine gun and artillery emplacements as the infantrymen moved forward. Close behind the infantry came the combat engineers who cleared and improved roads, sometimes under enemy fire, so that tanks and supplies could be brought forward. The next week of fighting saw a pattern develop. During the day, the 163rd continued the uphill attacks from the day before, advanced as far as they could with the assistance of tanks, bombers, and artillery, withstood any counter attacks, and established defensive perimeters. They then spent nervous nights anticipating and repelling Japanese night attacks.[40]

Company G had held its position on March 15, acting as an anchor for the attacks of other units, but on the 16th they received word that the Japanese were retreating and launched a two-pronged attack on the Japanese trenches and bunkers in front of them.[41] The men were ordered forward to locate fixed Japanese positions by drawing enemy fire and then tanks were brought up to destroy the enemy positions. This action resulted in the company's lead platoons being caught in the open under the guns of a significant enemy force while its scouts inched forward. The entire company hit the ground and sought shelter as Japanese mortar rounds fell on their positions. Once again, the tanks were called forward and within twenty minutes they had silenced the Japanese guns.[42] One of those tanks had been fitted with a bulldozer blade which it used to collapse an enemy pillbox burying the Japanese soldiers alive. The tank sat atop of the destroyed enemy position as the enemy soldiers cried out in pain.[43] Company G resumed their attack but were once again stopped by heavy mortar, machine-gun, and artillery fire. The company returned to the position it had held on March 15 for the night, which must have been depressing. One member of the company had been killed and others had suffered minor injuries.[44]

Tanks played a major role in American success at Zamboanga. Because there were no Japanese tanks in the area the only danger to American tanks came from Japanese artillery. To protect the tanks, Bruce and the other men of Company G moved forward to draw enemy artillery fire. This allowed scout planes to locate the Japanese artillery so that bombers and fighter bombers could take out the Japanese artillery allowing the American tanks to move forward safely. This proved to

Members of the 2nd Battalion of the 163rd caught in the open by Japanese artillery near Pasonanca, March 1945. (National Archives)

be very effective, but Bruce resented being used as a decoy to draw enemy fire.[45]

On March 17, in conjunction with Company E on their right Company G moved to push the Japanese off the ridges overlooking the town of Pasonanca.[46] They moved forward expecting more of the resistance they faced in the days before, but instead they found that the Japanese had abandoned their defenses and moved farther into the hills and jungles. The men advanced past abandoned guns, equipment, and the corpses of hundreds of enemy soldiers.[47] This was in part due to the effectiveness of U.S. artillery and airstrikes that cleared the way for their advance.

On March 18, in conjunction with Company E, Company G moved up the jungle ridges encountering and killing remnants of the retreating Japanese units.[48] A scouting patrol located a deserted Japanese headquarters

148 •   MACARTHUR'S BLOODY BUTCHERS

facility complete with an electronic switchboard rigged to blow up more
mines buried in the hills which the scouts destroyed but saw no enemy
soldiers. Another forward patrol surprised four Japanese soldiers on top
of another hill and killed all four before returning to report. When the
main body of the company reached the location the bodies of the four
Japanese soldiers had been removed indicating the presence of a substantial
number of enemy soldiers in the area. Even more disconcerting was the
company's discovery that a large gap had opened between them and
companies from the 162nd Regiment on their left which left Company
G in an exposed position at the end of the 163rd's line of advance.[49]

During their deployment in the Philippines the men of Company G
encountered more non-combatants and civilians than they had in New
Guinea and Biak. Though most of the time the people they encountered
were on their side the GIs were sometimes suspicious of some of the
people they met. On the afternoon of March 18, as Company G began to
set up their perimeter for the night an American missionary woman and
two Filipino men came down from their mission in the higher ground
and spoke with some members of the company before returning to their
mission. Based on the events that followed during the night of the 18th
Doyle Bruce believed they had passed information about Company G's
location to the enemy.[50]

That night the Japanese launched a substantial night attack on Company
G's perimeter.[51] At 12:30 a.m. Japanese soldiers attempted to silently
infiltrate the company's position, but alert GIs heard their approach and
set a trap for them. When the Japanese drew close enough, the Company
G men opened fire killing three of them and wounding their leader who
then blew himself up with a grenade. The Company G shooting drew
the attention of a Company H machine gunner dug in at an adjacent
position who laid down a steady stream of fire in front of Company G's
position, mowing down large numbers of Japanese soldiers. When a
Japanese machine gun opened fire on the Company H gunner, a Company
G BAR man killed the Japanese gun crew. In some places fighting was
hand-to-hand, and one American was wounded by a samurai sword
-wielding Japanese officer. A single Japanese soldier carrying explosives
broke through the perimeter and rushed toward Company HQ but was
brought down by rifle fire short of his goal. Several Americans were

wounded, and one killed in the night attack. Japanese casualties and deaths were much higher.[52]

On the night of the 18th, Bruce told his foxhole buddy that he had not had his boots off in a week and that he was going to sleep without them on the outside of their foxhole. He and two other men who followed his lead were sleeping on open ground when the big Japanese night attack began. The Japanese soldier with a large amount of TNT that ran through Company G's perimeter almost stepped on Bruce's face on his way to try to blow up the company headquarters. He failed, but Bruce was trapped outside his foxhole afraid to stand up and run back to safety because of the amount of rifle and machine-gun fire flying overhead. He and the other men managed to crawl into a small depression that offered them some amount of protection, but Bruce broke his toe crawling around. He spent the entire fire fight lying on his belly.[53] He was lucky not to be wounded by enemy or friendly fire. The next few days of fighting put Bruce and the other members of Company G in one dangerous position after another.

After closing the gap between themselves and the 162nd, Company G and the rest of the 163rd spent the next few days forming a continuous front relentlessly driving the Japanese from their defenses.[54] As a member of the company's 2nd Platoon Hargis Westerfield and the members of his squad were assigned to clear the Japanese from the jungle surrounding their position while another squad of men worked to clear the area of mines and booby traps. A Japanese sniper shot one of those men and a Japanese machine gun strafed the company's main position. Another member of 2nd Platoon was wounded and trapped in an area that made it seem impossible to rescue him. A sergeant and a BAR man and two other men moved forward to try to get to the wounded man. The BAR man fired several bursts into the area where the sergeant believed the enemy soldiers controlling the area were hiding. He gave the Japanese a few minutes to get away before moving forward to rescue the wounded GI. The plan worked and they reached the wounded man. He had been shot several times and had lost a good deal of blood, but he survived. By the end of the day Company G's 2nd Platoon had three men killed and several wounded or sickened. Its effective fighting strength had been reduced to just sixteen men.[55]

On March 19, Bruce and the weapons platoon moved forward with the main body of Company G to begin an uphill attack toward a group of pillboxes. The Japanese had 20mm and 40mm guns on the hilltop that they were pointing down the hill and using as artillery pieces. As Bruce crawled forward under heavy fire, he felt a blow hit his back like a sledgehammer. A large shell fragment had flown between his back and his pack. It tracked across his back at just the right angle so that it did not penetrate his skin, but instead left a large bruise and a burn all down his back. He told a buddy he had been hit but that he could make it back to the medics without help. He missed the rest of the attack but was back with the company the next day and participated in the fighting during the next several days. The back wound was Bruce's second and earned him an Oak Leaf Cluster addition to his Purple Heart Medal. The wounds Bruce sustained helped him qualify for a quicker rotation home, but he had to make a few more landings and go on a few more combat patrols before that happened.[56]

On March 20, Company G and the rest of the 163rd resumed their uphill assault. Westerfield's depleted 2nd Platoon entered a steep-sided valley that Japanese forces had withdrawn from overnight. By the morning the Filipino villagers were already returning to their homes and they gave the Americans fresh eggs and vegetables as they moved through. 2nd Platoon held their position as men from Company F moved through them from their forward position carrying members of their unit that had been killed. They gave dire reports of the area ahead of Company G being dotted with more pillboxes than they could count. Despite the grim news, Company G received orders to move forward. An advanced patrol moved to take positions on the high ground on the left side of the valley while a squad from Company E did the same on the right. When they reached their positions the rest of Company G moved through those advanced positions to begin the attack. They only covered one hundred yards before Japanese machine gun and rifle fire pinned them down. 2nd Platoon's BAR man returned fire on the pillbox from which the machine-gun fire was coming but failed to knock it out. The men of 2nd Platoon remained pinned down until heavy machine guns could be brought forward to cover their retreat. Even then only enough covering fire could be provided to allow one man to withdraw at a time.

The company was ordered to dig in on the high ground at the opening of the valley where they felt like sitting ducks. Their position seemed to be surrounded by the enemy and vulnerable to attack from positions higher up than theirs. When the Japanese cut their communication wire, their exposure became obvious to battalion command who ordered them to retreat to their position from the night before. They had to make do with K rations for dinner because their company cooks had been fired on as they tried to approach, but at least they were in a less dangerous situation.[57]

Because the full force of the 162nd and 163rd Regiments were being thrown against enemy positions in the hills around Pasonanca, the Japanese often found that they had to retreat from positions they had effectively defended the day before or have those positions cut off by the advance of Americans elsewhere. March 21 began with Company G advancing through the village they had passed through the day before, driving a few Japanese soldiers from the positions they had occupied during the night, and moving past the place at the valley opening where they had been stopped on March 20. They reached the bottom of a hill that they called "Coconut Hill" without major incident. With 2nd Platoon acting as base, 1st and 3rd Platoons began their assault up the hill. They were met with heavy rifle, machine-gun, and mortar fire that stopped their advance. A soldier named Hoffman died in the attack before it was called off.[58]

By the time Hargis Westerfield landed with Company G on the beaches of Mindanao near Zamboanga City on March 10, 1945, he was a hardened veteran of the Aitape, Wakde, and Biak campaigns. And, though he wrote about his experiences at Zamboanga years after the events took place, his descriptions of those events are those of a man tired of war, inured to the dangers of combat, and preoccupied with death. His account of the fighting at Zamboanga makes for grim reading.

Westerfield found much to complain about during the fighting at Zamboanga: the ramp of the landing craft that took his platoon to the beach malfunctioned, there were not enough Japanese to kill in the first few days, a recon outfit let the company walk into a firestorm of mortar and artillery fire, and on. But mostly he recorded details of the deaths of his comrades: Private Thomas Bradley killed by rifle fire, Private First Class Kenneth Marsh killed by a 20mm shell that struck him in the side, Private David McCorkle killed by a direct hit of a mortar shell, Lieutenant Frank Messenger killed when he stepped on a land mine, Private Eugene Bombardier killed by mortar shrapnel, Sergeant Raymond Utgard killed by a grenade during the Japanese night attack, Sergeant Stanley Fields killed in a hail of machine-gun fire while trying to save company scout Private Anthony Fiorello, and Private Kenneth Hoffman shot in the forehead during the attack on "Coconut Hill."[59]

The death of Hoffman affected Westerfield the most because he was assigned to the group sent to recover his body the day after he was killed. When Westerfield and the others found Hoffman's body, it was still in the kneeling position he had been in when he was shot. The bullet had only left a small hole in his forehead. The Company G detail carried Hoffman in their arms down the mud-sided hills in heavy rain. On the way they witnessed another GI fall to a sniper's bullet, and they carried him to safety. The bullet lodged near his spine, but he lived. It was not until the next day that the company priest could come forward to retrieve Hoffman's body and perform the last rites. Westerfield rode to the rear in the truck with the body. Many years later he described a memorable interaction that took place during the trip. As he bumped along in the back of the truck next to Hoffman's blanket-covered body, Westerfield questioned the point of the war and the useless way in which so many men died. At one point the truck stopped to pick up a family of Filipino refugees carrying all their possessions, including a live chicken. The young son of the family, at first boisterous, made eye contact with Westerfield, who pointed at Hoffman's body. The little boy became quiet and removed his hat. This act of reverence reminded Westerfeld that the war was not without purpose.[60]

Company G maneuvered to occupy a hill near "Coconut Hill" on March 22 while an artillery barrage and aerial bombing runs pounded the Japanese positions on and around it. One of the Marine Corsairs mistook Company G's hilltop position for his target and unleashed a 500-pound bomb. Watching from a distance, battalion command was convinced that the bomb had wiped out Company G. Fortunately, the bomb carried just over a ridge into a valley before detonating. It left the men of Company G shattered but unscathed and they were ordered to stop their advance for the day.[61]

On the 23rd Company G's attack resumed, and their objective was "Coconut Hill." They advanced in a line across the hill where the bomb had narrowly missed them and then across one hundred yards of semi-open territory. They were met with a smattering of mortar fire before beginning their attack up the slopes of the hill. On their way up they stopped to inspect two caves, one of which contained an abandoned Japanese 20mm gun. As they examined the cave area mortar shells fell among them. The only one that could have done any damage malfunctioned and did not explode. Using squad-based tactics in which one squad established a firebase to cover the advance of another, Company G took "Coconut Hill," killing the few Japanese defenders that remained in the otherwise abandoned shelters on its top.

They remained in that position on the 24th and were relieved by Company B on the 25th. They boarded trucks that took them back to their former positions at Santa Maria where they enjoyed food prepared by the company's kitchen detail and the chance to wash and put on clean clothes for a few days before being deployed for their next assignment.[62]

By March 24, most of the Pasonanca Valley had been secured and the men of the 163rd Regiment began to be relieved by other units.[63] They had been in continuous combat in forward positions against a determined enemy fighting from prepared defensive positions for two weeks. Casualties among the 1st and 2nd Battalions were high with several companies missing a third to a half of their men.[64]

On June 12, 1945, members of the 61st Infantry Regiment captured the diary of a Japanese officer named Ryosuke Maya near the Philippine village of Mialim on the island of Mindanao. Lieutenant Maya belonged to an air brigade but within a few days of the American invasion of Zamboanga, he was placed under the command of the 5th Infantry Brigade. The first entry was made on February 7, the day Lieutenant Maya arrived at Zamboanga, and the last on June 5. The diary is a record not just of the military actions of the Japanese forces on Mindanao, but a record of the disillusionment and suffering of Lieutenant Maya as the Japanese military situation on the island deteriorated.

His diary entry for March 8 reported news of the approaching American invasion fleet which, combined with bombing from a variety of American aircraft, convinced the Japanese command that an invasion in their area was imminent. The next day Maya recorded that carrier-based planes began bombing Japanese positions at 7:00 am, followed by a naval bombardment that began at 10:00 a.m. and lasted two hours, followed by more aerial bombing by what Maya estimated were fifty B-24s. Maya also included an erroneous report that Japanese forces had repelled an attempted American landing. Maya and his men were ordered to withdraw from the airstrip where they were stationed to join the brigade's headquarters company—a move that was made during a period of heavy bombardment.

March 10 was the day that the 162nd and 163rd Infantry Regiments landed at Zamboanga, but Maya didn't witness the landing because the headquarters unit he had been attached to continued its withdrawal into the prepared Japanese defenses on the high ground to the north of Zamboanga City.

The next day Maya shared his assessment of the American invasion. He estimated that the invading U.S. force consisted of 2,500 men, 120 tanks, and 60 trucks. Maya's assessment of the Japanese military situation was optimistic. He credited a Japanese night assault with stopping the American advance and increasing the American military reliance on artillery and tanks. He remained optimistic through March 12, though he noted some ominous signs of American success and progress. American observation planes were already taking off and landing from the airstrips U.S. forces had seized in the early days of the invasion and American engineering units were already at work repairing those airstrips so they could be made even more useful. Maya's entry of the 13th claimed that the Japanese had only suffered 250 casualties and had destroyed forty American tanks.

By the time Maya wrote his March 14 entry, all his optimism was gone. Assigned to a lookout post on a hilltop, Maya had a clear view of the progress of the American military at Zamboanga. He saw American engineering units working to extend and improve runways and was infuriated when that work continued under bright lights throughout the night because the Americans were so confident of their safety. He also noted that after only four days of fighting, the advanced American units had already reached the first line of prepared defenses and that threw Japanese headquarters into a panic as they prepared to withdraw to a safer position in the jungle highlands. Maya disapproved of this move and stated that he was still ready to die in the line of duty.

Things deteriorated for Maya and his men in their advanced lookout position over the next five days as the 162nd and 163rd Regiments began moving through Japanese positions. Maya and his men spent most of March 15 taking shelter from steady American mortar fire. On March 16, they were relieved and rejoined the headquarters unit. Maya reported that the position of the Japanese had become increasingly unfavorable and that all Japanese units had suffered considerable casualties from U.S. mortar and artillery fire. His entry of March 20 described the situation in even bleaker terms, and he reported that the headquarters unit was preparing to retreat even farther into the hills and jungle. At 7:00 a.m. the next morning Maya and his men began a four-mile hike to their new position in a heavy rainstorm. And then on March 22, one of the last days of combat for Company G of the 163rd Regiment's 2nd Battalion, Maya wrote that it appeared that the Japanese had abandoned all their defensive positions in the hills to the north of Zamboanga City. On March 23, Maya's entry expressed little hope for his unit's future and described plans for a suicide mission that had been discussed amongst the men. In the end they decided that such an attack would hurt the overall Japanese mission and they decided to wait to join other units in a large counteroffensive. Maya felt some despair about the situation in which he and his men found themselves, but he continued to believe that the Japanese military could still turn things around. The large counteroffensive he and his men waited for never happened.

For the next three months, Lieutenant Maya's diary is a record of almost constant movement, physical suffering, despair, and hunger as he and his comrades ran low on supplies and tried to avoid both American military units and groups of Filipino freedom fighters. From time to time his entries also contained insights into the Japanese military, assessments of the U.S. military, and the mindset of the two opposing forces. On March 27, Maya wrote that American infantry units only advanced under the cover of an artillery barrage which allowed them to move deep into enemy positions. He and his men had learned that these artillery barrages meant that the U.S. soldiers would be making rapid advances and taking over places that Japanese commanders could not have expected. If Maya had a grudging respect for the efficiency of the American military, he did not have a high opinion of their methods or of the fighting spirit of the American soldiers—Maya described the American military's methods as insincere and unusual. He felt that attacks made by American soldiers lacked urgency and fighting spirit. Apparently, the American military's desire to keep American casualties low made Maya doubt the American military's decision-making.

The next week's entries were filled with records of long marches on light rations while carrying heavy burdens as the Japanese military continued its evacuation of the area around Zamboanga. On April 5, Maya reported that the large number of casualties suffered by all the Japanese units were impeding the progress of his unit's marches. The next day he and his men hiked eight kilometers without water. Maya's diary entries show his mounting frustration and exhaustion with the long marches and the constant rain that made his suffering worse. But for Maya sitting still was worse than moving. As an officer he had some idea of how far they had to go and how limited their supplies were, which convinced him that every day not moving was a waste. It was when they were stationary that Maya noticed the deterioration of his men and their equipment. On April 15, he wrote that his sword blade had sustained several nicks while cutting palm for a shelter and that his pistol was covered with rust.

By late April, tension had developed between units of Japanese Marines and army units and the two branches decided to separate and go their own way. By this time all the Japanese units were spending a great deal of time foraging for food. Occasional engagements with Filipino resistance fighters and sightings of U.S. observation planes kept the Japanese soldiers on high alert, and they were frequently bombed and strafed by U.S. planes. Sickness and hunger continued to be a problem, but on April 29 Maya did what he could to observe the Japanese emperor's birthday by praying fervently for the emperor's continued health and long life.

As U.S. forces and Filipino fighters closed in, foraging became much more dangerous for Maya and the other Japanese. In the early days of May, Maya's spirits rose briefly as his unit was joined by several of the other Japanese units scattered across Mindanao. On May 10 the food crisis reached its peak when all units ran out. The lack of food led to increased desertions and the breakdown of military discipline. To Maya they had only two options: they could escape to the east coast of the island or attack the Americans in the hope of acquiring food. Maya favored the move to the east and requested permission to lead what remained of his air unit to the east coast, but his request was denied by General Tokichi Hojo.

The rest of May was spent in a misery of long marches and foraging parties that resulted in high casualties and rarely reduced hunger. Men who could not keep up were shot and killed. Maya woke on May 20 with a fever, chills, and a terrible headache. During that day's march, he considered dropping out and accepting his fate but managed to make it through the day. At a meeting of all the commanding officers on May 23, General Hojo announced that each unit was on its own and could pursue whatever course of action they thought best. Lieutenant Maya decided that he and his remaining nine men would join a battalion headed for the east coast. Encounters with American forces, disease, and hunger continued to claim the lives of the men in Maya's group. By the end of the month the battalion was lost and down to fewer than sixty men. Maya's last diary entries were short and poignant.

On June 1 and 2, he recorded that he and his men were still marching to the east and that conditions for the men were very difficult. On June 3 and 4 he reported that they still had not reached their destination and were out of food. His last entry was made on June 5, when he wrote that he believed their coastal destination was in sight and that he was sad because they had had to leave a corporal behind because he could no longer keep up with the group.[65]

No record of what became of Lieutenant Maya remains.

CHAPTER II

The Sulu Archipelago

April 21, 1945–July 4, 1945

By the time Doyle Bruce crawled into the amphibious vehicle that would take him across the straits from Tawi Tawi to the island of Bongao in the Sulu Archipelago, very little made an impression on him, and he recorded almost nothing about Company G's actions on the island group. The only combat incident he remembered was accidentally walking in the open in front of a known Japanese position. War had become routine for him and for most of the veterans of Company G.[1]

The 41st Division's landings at Palawan and Zamboanga, and their subsequent seizure of both, drew praise for the division and its leaders from General MacArthur. The amphibious assaults had gone almost exactly as planned and the reduction of the Japanese defenses, while costly, had been handled with skill and efficiency. As the fighting on Mindanao shifted away from the Zamboanga Peninsula to Sibuko Bay and the interior of the island, Division Headquarters moved into an old Spanish Fort in Zamboanga City.[2]

Fighting on Mindanao continued into the summer of 1945, but instead of fighting alongside one another as they had at Zamboanga, the individual regiments of the division fought independently. Elements of the 186th Regiment took over for the 163rd and continued to press the attack against the Japanese in the hills and jungles above Zamboanga City, while the 186th Regiment's 2nd Battalion made a long, looping westward move to land at Sibuko Bay, behind the main Japanese defenses.

The 162nd Regiment continued its push up the Zamboanga Peninsula as well, driving the Japanese toward the 2nd Battalion of the 186th.

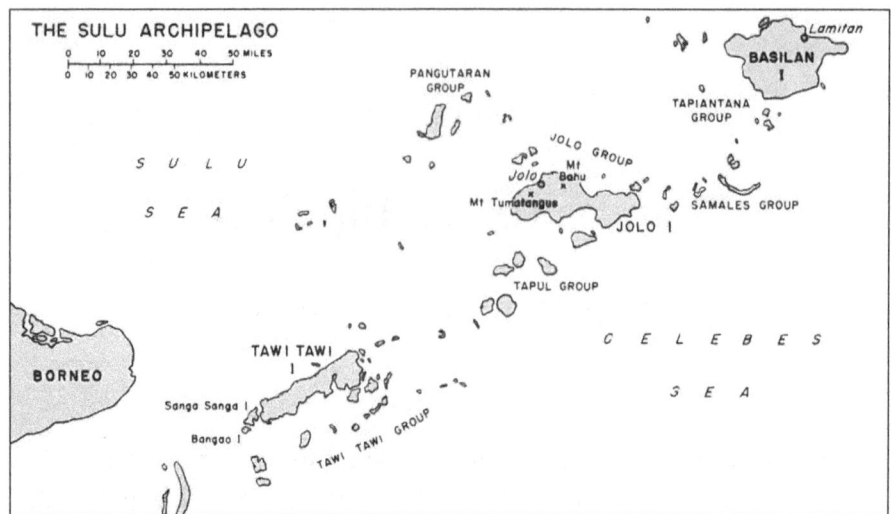

Map of the Sulu Archipelago. Sanga Sanga and Bongao where Company G landed are located at the far western end of the island chain. (U.S. Army Center of Military History)

The regiment's Company F began the division's next line of attack by capturing Basilan Island in the Sulu Archipelago. Arranged like a series of steppingstones connecting Mindanao to Borneo, the Sulu Archipelago harbored substantial Japanese forces and was strategically important to the Japanese and the allied forces. Following these actions, the 162nd joined XX Corps for their drive into central Mindanao working with the 21st and 31st Divisions as they drove the remaining Japanese defenders on the island deeper into the jungle, destroying them as they went as part of MacArthur's Victor V Plan for retaking the Philippines. The 163rd Regiment concentrated its efforts on capturing the remaining islands in the Sulu Archipelago.[3]

On April 2, 1945, the 163rd Regiment began its fight for control of the Sulu Archipelago with the 2nd Battalion landing in the Tawi Tawi group of islands at the far western end of the archipelago. Their objective was the seizure of an airstrip on the island of Sanga Sanga across from a major Japanese navy facility and then the destruction of the Japanese garrisons wherever they might be found. Constant attacks from Filipino guerillas in the Tawi Tawi group and supply shortages had reduced military readiness of the Japanese defenses in advance of the 2nd Battalion's move, making the accomplishment of their objective easier.

The Sulu White Task Force, with the 2nd Battalion as its primary combat unit, a field artillery group, combat engineers, a platoon of amphibious vehicles, and medical unit, left Zamboanga on March 31 accompanied by the destroyers *Phillips* and *Waller*, headed for the island of Sanga Sanga with the 419 Night Fighter Squadron providing air cover. An airstrip on the island across from a largely abandoned Japanese naval base on Tawi Tawi was their objective. The task force arrived off the coast of the island early on the morning of April 2. The jungle surrounding the beach designated as the landing zone for 2nd Battalion had been subjected to an aerial bombardment from American bombers that dropped heavy ordnance on the Japanese defenses for ten days in the lead up to the landing.

2nd Battalion's move accomplished several objectives. It laid the groundwork for the Jolo invasion that would take place in the following days. Their quick and efficient action also cut off a route of retreat for the Japanese garrison on Jolo and provided the jumping off point for an Australian Army-led invasion of nearby Borneo and the reduction of the large Japanese base there. They were aided by the active and courageous Filipino rebels on the islands who had been waging guerilla warfare on the Japanese for years, but the operation demonstrated just how effective a veteran unit with coordinated air, naval, and artillery support could be.[4]

Even before Company G embarked for Sanga Sanga with the rest of the Sulu White Task Force, its role as the lead unit in the invasion of the Island of Bongao had been determined. Company commander Captain Braman had flown in a reconnaissance mission above the island while his company remained on the Zamboanga Peninsula. Aboard the landing craft that ferried the men of the task force to their landing zone on Sanga Sanga, the men of Company G watched as a flight of American Liberator bombers streamed over head to drop their 500-pound bombs ahead of the invasion. A squadron of Marine Corsairs followed the bombers and dropped their lighter ordnance with the intent of easing the infantry landing by destroying Japanese defenses and defenders. At the same time, the guns aboard U.S. destroyers *Phillips* and *Waller* sought out Japanese artillery emplacements on the island.[5]

As the landing craft carrying the 2nd Battalion approached, the Filipino rebels who had driven the Japanese from the base on Tawi Tawi, and who the U.S. military had been supplying and receiving intelligence from for years, waded out into the surf waving an American flag. The Filipino rebels who greeted them from the surf informed them that all the Japanese defenders of Tawi Tawi and Sanga Sanga had retreated to defensive positions on Bongao.[6] Their efforts and the American preparation meant that the landing on Sanga Sanga drew no enemy fire, allowing the 2nd Battalion to land and unload their equipment and support units with no casualties. After securing the beach, the battalion's four companies moved inland and secured the airstrip.[7]

The next objective was landing on nearby Bongao Island and destroying the mixed unit Japanese defenders there. Within an hour of landing Company G boarded the "Alligator" amphibious vehicles to cross the straight separating Sanga Sanga from Bongoa. Another Marine bombing run pummeled the jungle around the Americans' landing zone. Company G set off for the island behind a screen of rolling artillery fire with Companies E and H following. No enemy resistance slowed their progress and Company G secured the beach allowing the other Task Force companies to land. The company then headed inland in search of the enemy while the other companies did the same. Only Company E encountered any significant Japanese resistance. Before nightfall all three companies had gained their objectives, dug perimeter defenses, and settled in for the night. Some positions took mortar and sniper fire in the late afternoon but there were no casualties.[8] A Japanese 20mm gun shelled the landing area on Sanga Sanga where elements of the 146th Field Artillery were unloading their guns but again there were no casualties.[9]

The location of the American landings on April 2, and the speed and efficiency with which the U.S. military moved against Bongao, forced the Japanese to abandon their coastal defenses and Bongao Port. By the end of the first day of action Company G still had not encountered any Japanese defenders and held a position at a crossroads of two trails: one that led from the two Japanese strongholds on the hills and high grounds of Bongao's interior and one that led down to Bongao Port. Joined by

Company E and a platoon of heavy machine guns from Company H, the men of Company G dug perimeter defenses facing both directions along the crossroads and settled in for the evening. In the late afternoon, Japanese snipers and mortars fired a few rounds at the American position, but there were no casualties.

At 9:00 p.m. the Japanese launched a counterattack against the American position at the crossroads. To the men of Company G, it seemed that the Japanese had misjudged the location of their position in the darkness because Japanese rifle fire seemed to be aimed past the Americans. Machine guns from the Company H platoon, stationed at the crossroads, opened up and raked the jungle in the direction of the Japanese fire while the men of G and E Companies threw grenades at any sound of movement around their position. The Japanese attack did not last long and there were no American casualties. In the morning, a Company G patrol found the bodies of seven dead Japanese soldiers along the trail leading towards Mount Kabogan.[10] Many of the dead Japanese soldiers had carried new rifles indicating that the defenders of Bongao had been recently resupplied.[11]

Companies G and E spent April 3 patrolling the island in search of the enemy and, in the process, securing strong strategic positions. Despite extensive patrols by Company G platoons that covered both the east and west ends of the island they encountered no Japanese soldiers. They did find large stores of abandoned supplies further reinforcing the idea that the Japanese on the island, wherever they were, were well supplied. Patrols from Company E moved into Bongao Port and, though they found mess facilities and barracks loaded with supplies, they did not encounter any enemy soldiers. With the coast of Bongao literally clear, Company G, Company H, and Company E, minus one rifle platoon and its weapons platoon, moved into Bongao Port and the area around it. Company G established its position on a small rise just outside the town. Their evening passed in more comfort and with more merriment than most nights spent in combat areas. The company's cooks prepared hot food and the men shared two bottles of whiskey, as well as some Japanese beer, and a case of soda that one of their patrols had liberated from a Japanese barracks.

Sobriety returned quickly during the night when Japanese machine guns and rifles opened fire from one of their positions in the hills above Bongao Port on a Filipino guerilla group that had lit fires at their camp site. The Japanese overshot their intended target and stray bullets whizzed through Company G's encampment. One of the company's BAR men caught a round in his buttocks, but he was the only casualty in the unexpected night attack.[12]

Patrols spread out from the 2nd Battalion positions on the morning of April 4 in search of the enemy. A patrol that reached the edge of Bongao Port found abandoned Japanese gun emplacements, barracks, and mess facilities but drew only light machine-gun fire from positions in the hills behind the town. Instead of focusing their counterattack on the American forces already ashore, the Japanese launched a counterattack against elements of the 146 Field Artillery as they crossed from Sanga Sanga to Bongao killing one American. On April 4, elements of Company G returned to action. An undermanned platoon received orders to take out a 20mm Japanese artillery position located on a hill adjacent to Mount Kabogan. As a squad began the ascent up the slope of the hill, they received word from an observation plane that the Japanese position appeared to be abandoned. With this information the squad climbed the hill and moved into the position without incident. They found four Japanese 20mm guns damaged and abandoned and killed the only Japanese soldier they encountered. They also found three cases of beer which they quickly divided among themselves and drank.

From the position on the hill, the Marine forward observer who accompanied the Company G platoon had an ideal vantage point from which to direct Marine Air Corps bombing runs on the Japanese position in the hills around them. Three flights of Corsairs unleashed their bombs on the Japanese position which was Company G's next objective. A bombardment from the 146th Field Artillery followed the Marine bombing runs as the men of the company worked their way up steep slopes and through rolls of Japanese barbed wire toward their objective. When they reached the enemy position, they found only the mangled bodies of Japanese defenders.

Men of 2nd Battalion of the 163rd Infantry advance through Bongao Port, April 1945. (National Archives)

The destruction of the Japanese artillery paved the way for an infantry assault on the main Japanese defensive positions on Mount Kabogan. The men of the 2nd Battalion overran the Japanese defenses on the 706-foot-high peak with little resistance, finding few enemy soldiers in those positions either alive or dead. After receiving orders to press their attack up Mount Kabogan, Company G trudged through dense jungle, ravines, and up steep slopes of the mountain to a height of just over 700 feet. The Japanese position, which was their objective still lay above them. A squad ordered to find the way up the slope to the Japanese positions discovered a group of enemy soldiers. Ineffective rifle fire from these Japanese soldiers followed the Company G scouts as they returned from their mission. The slopes of Mount Kabogan were honeycombed with caves in which battalion command determined the main body of the Japanese defenders were hiding.[13]

Battalion command waited until April 5 to pursue the Japanese into the ravines and jungles on the slopes of the mountain. Led to a cave with an opening in the slope of a ravine by a Japanese civilian prisoner, the Americans again hesitated to attack. They believed there could be up to 300 Japanese soldiers defending the cave and they were not entirely sure that their Japanese prisoner had not led them into a trap. On April 6, the Americans attacked the Japanese position, but steady Japanese rifle and machine-gun fire tore through the GIs struggling to carry their attack up the steep slopes leading to the cave. Following this unsuccessful assault, regimental command made the decision to wait the Japanese out and not risk any more American lives in attacks. While the Japanese soldiers hiding in the cave and the surrounding areas were well supplied with ammunition and food, they lacked access to fresh water. Filipino guerillas on the island were told to garrison the freshwater points on Bongao and kill the Japanese who were driven by desperate thirst to come out of their defensive positions. Through this cruel war of attrition, the remaining Japanese defenders were destroyed.[14]

Ironically, one Company G platoon had the only real encounter with the enemy during the entire operation after the attack was called off. As the platoon moved down the mountain slopes to spend the night at the crossroads position established on the first day of the attack on Bongao, they ran across an undiscovered pocket of Japanese soldiers only a few hundred yards from the crossroads. Two Japanese soldiers were on the trail, one laying down on the ground and the other sitting near him. When the Americans ordered them to put their hands up, the soldier on the ground indicated that there were more Japanese soldiers hiding in the jungle. That soldier then made a sudden move and was shot to death. The other soldier tried to run and was cut down as well. A third Japanese soldier who had remained unseen in the jungle also tried to run and was killed. Following the direction provided by the Japanese soldier who had died lying on the ground, the platoon moved farther up the trail where they discovered yet another Japanese soldier. The platoon opened fire on him, but he escaped under the cover of rifle fire from other Japanese soldiers hidden just inside the jungle. The platoon leader ordered some of his men to lay down a base of fire while the rest of the platoon moved forward throwing grenades into the jungle where they believed the enemy was hiding. They then charged the Japanese position.

In a trench just inside the jungle fringe they found and killed five more enemy soldiers. This incident was the last significant combat action the company experienced on Bongao and is a good example of the type of fighting at which the men of Company G had become expert: small, quick, deadly actions against enemy soldiers encountered in unexpected places with no quarter given.[15]

With the extreme southern end of the Sulu Archipelago under American control, U.S. military planners turned their attention to the island of Jolo, the largest and most important island in the chain. In coordination with the 163rd's move down the archipelago there were daily air raids by American bombers and fighter bombers. Then on April 8, the other two battalions of the 163rd landed on the beaches of Jolo. The 3rd Battalion landed first securing the beachhead for the 1st Battalion which followed them on shore. The 1st Battalion quickly moved into Jolo City while the 3rd Battalion moved inland to attack the Japanese who had withdrawn to their prepared defensive positions on the high ground in the interior of the island. The 2nd Battalion combat companies withdrew from Bongoa and joined the rest of the 163rd on Jolo on April 10 where they took part in the fight for control of that island.[16]

The mountainous geography of Jolo provided excellent defensive positions and the Japanese commander took full advantage of the terrain. Like the Japanese commander at Zamboanga, he had largely abandoned his coastal defenses and moved his men, and the equipment they could take with them, to higher ground. The arrival of the 2nd Battalion on April 10 freed up the 1st and 3rd Battalions to begin their attacks on the Japanese positions in the island's interior.[17]

The 1st and 3rd Battalions launched their attacks against the Japanese defenses beginning on April 12. The 1st Battalion operating to the west encountered the heaviest enemy opposition on the trails approaching Mount Daho while the 3rd attacked the Japanese forces on Mount Magusing. Despite tough fighting both battalions achieved their objectives and moved into position to attack the Japanese on Mount Daho. There 400 Japanese defenders occupied the trenches, pillboxes, and bunkers on the mountain's slopes. The ridges and ravines gave them a significant defensive advantage and the Japanese commander planned to use those advantages to make the Americans pay for every inch of ground and for each defender's life that they took. The American operations against Mount Daho began on April 16 with an attack by 1st Battalion.[18] Despite their geographic advantage, the Japanese garrison on Jolo was weak. They had not been resupplied for six months and the soldiers who made up the garrison came from units that had been broken up and reassigned. Many of those units were rear echelon and their soldiers had no combat experience. Hungry, sick, and without hope of resupply, naval, or air support, they sat in their trenches and waited for the American attack.[19]

Four days of artillery bombardment and thirty-six bombing runs by U.S. Marine fighter bombers pummeled the Japanese defenders on Mount Daho before 1st Battalion resumed its push up the mountain on April 20.

Soldiers of the 163rd scramble for cover during their advance through high ground on the island of Jolo, April 1945. (National Archives)

Despite the devastating bombardment, the Japanese unleashed volleys of withering rifle and small arms fire at the Americans scrambling uphill, killing three men, and wounding an additional twenty-nine. Offensive operations halted on April 21 to coordinate air support for the next attack. Prior to a resumption of 1st Battalion's attack on April 22, the Japanese defenders on Daho received another crippling field artillery bombardment as well as bombardment from a flight of thirty-seven U.S. bombers that reduced their position to rubble and killed 235 men. The Japanese soldiers who survived the bombardment broke as the 1st Battalion attack began and fled to Mount Tumatangas where they joined other Japanese who had been driven or fled from other positions on the island. They would make their last stand there.[20]

If anything, Mount Tumatangas offered even better defensive positions than Mount Daho. Most of the remaining Japanese defenders of Jolo gathered there and dug in along the lip of a crater that made up the highest ridge of the mountain. The crater stretched for 600 yards, was more than 300-yards-wide and fell to a depth of 300 feet in places. From their position on the crater's edge the Japanese riflemen, machine gunners, and mortar men could look down over the ravines, jungle, and hills covered in tall grass that made up the approaches to Mount Tumatangas.

Third Battalion received orders to take the ridge on April 23 and Companies L, K, and I moved forward. Company L made easy progress under the cover of jungle canopy and behind a screen of mortar fire. They covered hundreds of yards in the initial phase of the advance. They discovered the remains of an old Spanish fortification built into the lower face of the mountain and destroyed it. A Company L patrol searched ahead in an attempt to link up with a position established by Company I. They established contact with Company I and returned but also reported the presence of Japanese soldiers in the area. The company commander decided to move forward toward the crater's edge. He plotted a route that would take Company L out into the open but would avoid having to hack and sweat their way through more dense jungle. Because the advance required the men to move up a steep slope, some men fell behind. When the main body of Company L stopped to let them catch up, they were raked by Japanese rifle and machine-gun fire from the high ground in front of them. The GIs scrambled for whatever cover they could find, but there was little to offer them any protection. Company L's commanding officer left the bulk of his men to hold their position while he and a few men rushed to Company I for reinforcements. Two members of the company died and ten members of the Company were wounded before he was able to return. Fighting continued on the slopes of Mount Tumatangas until June 30.[21]

By early May, the combat on Jolo had devolved into patrols that searched for pockets of Japanese defenders as a part of the mopping-up phase. The 2nd Battalion began taking part in these potentially deadly patrols in early May.[22]

By the time of the invasion of Bongao and Jolo, Private Westerfield had become accustomed to mud, filth, stink, killing, and death. Westerfield's report on one of Company G's patrols on Jolo provides frank insights into the effect combat against the Japanese had on the mind and attitudes of American soldiers.

On May 10, Company G pulled out of Jolo City to relieve Company K which had been holding a position on the slopes of Mount Tumatangas. Westerfield lamented leaving behind his Moro "girlfriend" in Jolo City and the thought of other soldiers making her acquaintance. Ribald jokes and reports of enemy activity in the area that the men of Company G heard from the unit they were replacing made the move even more unsettling for Westerfield and the others.

Westerfield's platoon moved into American trenches on the mountain slopes while other platoons patrolled the area on the first day. Not long after taking up their position they heard the report of an American carbine and a short while after that, a sergeant from one of the squads on patrol ran back to Westerfield's platoon's position. His squad had come across four Japanese soldiers sitting and smoking along the trail they were patrolling. They killed those four men and rushed forward to attack the enemy, killing seven more men and weakening the Japanese position. Because of their small number and their wounded, the squad could not continue the attack. The sergeant picked a few men to go with him back to his squad's position and Westerfield was one of them.

When the platoon Westerfield was a member of reached the American squad, he and three other men used a poncho for a makeshift litter to evacuate the most severely wounded man from the Japanese foxhole where the soldier had been wounded. After getting the man to safety, the reinforced squad continued the attack against the Japanese positions and successfully moved forward, capturing an area around a spring where they dug a trench on a ridge overlooking the enemy position. A supply party brought Westerfield's platoon rations that evening. He ate corned beef and crackers, and the members of his squad shared a can of peas which they primarily valued for the liquid. For dessert he ate an O'Henry bar that was made with real chocolate, not the altered chocolate normally used in candy meant for the soldiers fighting in the Pacific. He enjoyed his feast despite the presence of the rotting corpse of a Japanese soldier less than ten yards away.

After a breakfast of K rations, Westerfield filled his only canteen before the entire company moved out. This would prove to be very important in the days ahead. Company G spent the day doing grueling, terrifying climbs up and down ravines and through the close, suffocating atmosphere of dense jungles. Sometimes the slopes they scaled were so steep the men literally fought for hand and footholds and were forced to drag their equipment behind them, all the while praying that no Japanese snipers would spot them in that vulnerable position.

At the top of one of the ridges, Westerfield and his comrades found significant, recent signs of Japanese activity and posted pickets in case of an enemy attack. Not long before dark, one of the pickets fired his BAR and Westerfield and another man rushed forward. A Japanese grenade exploded nearby and in response Westerfield and the others sprayed the jungle in front of them with rifle fire. The man who rushed forward with Westerfield claimed to have killed a tall Japanese soldier in an opening in the jungle cover. Westerfield threw two grenades into the spot with no effect and then waited for more members of the squad to move forward to cover him as he crept ahead. When he stepped into the jungle, he found a wounded Japanese soldier in a foxhole and killed him with a grenade.

Westerfield and two other scouts searched ahead for a few yards before one of the other men swung toward a patch of jungle and emptied his M1. He yelled to Westerfield that the soldier he had fired on was not dead. Westerfield approached the place where the other man had fired and found a wounded Japanese officer who placed a small grenade on his chest and smiled before it detonated, killing himself but not injuring Westerfield or the others. He later realized that the Japanese officer had sacrificed himself by staying behind to buy time so his men could escape.

The company continued their advance to another hilltop position but found no Japanese soldiers alive or dead there. They dug a perimeter on the hilltop and settled in for the evening expecting to be resupplied with water by a carrying party. That party did not come, leaving the men of Company G who had spent a terrifying and arduous day climbing up and down in heat and humidity without water for the night. Most of the men spent the evening trying to drain the last drops from their canteens, but Westerfield fared a little better because he had filled his canteen that morning. The men who had spent most of the day without any water had to do the same for the night. The water crisis became worse the next

The Sultan of Sulu photographed by American forces on Jolo, 1945. (National Archives)

day when the carrying party that set out for their position with water was delayed by a counterattack against Company E's position and then pressed into service as stretcher bearers. Water finally reached Company G in the afternoon. The next day the company was relieved by Filipino rebels, and they returned to Jolo City. That patrol was the last combat action in which Company G took part—a fact Westerfield regretted.[23]

The presence of a large Muslim population added a layer of interest and tension to the 163rd's invasion of Jolo. Muhammed Janail Abirir was the Sultan of Jolo, which made him the political and religious leader of the Moro people who made up the majority of the inhabitants of the island. Establishing good relations with the Sultan and the Moros took priority in the days following the 163rd's landing. Regimental command met with the Sultan who had surrendered to American General John J. Pershing at the end of the U.S. war against the Moros in 1913 and still had a sword that General Pershing had given him. American efforts to establish good relations with the Sultan went well, aided in part by the harsh treatment the Sultan and his people had endured under Japanese control.[24]

An encounter with the Moros was what Doyle Bruce remembered as his most terrifying experience during Company G's actions in the Sulu Archipelago. Assigned to guard a group of Moros who were being held as prisoners because they were suspected of collaborating with the Japanese, Bruce and nine other men from Company G found themselves surrounded by a large group of Moro citizens who were relatives of the men being held prisoner. He feared that he and the other guards would be attacked and killed by the angry crowd. Fortunately for Bruce and the other guards, the good relations established with the Sultan and his people by the 163rd Regiment's leaders had earned the trust of the Moro people. Despite their unhappiness, the crowd backed off, but they did not leave. They camped out near the POW enclosure and waited for their friends and relatives to be released.[25]

The U.S. military success on Jolo came at a cost. Thirty-five American soldiers died during the three-plus months of fighting and 125 were wounded.[26]

Following the operation on Zamboanga and in the Sulu Archipelago, many of the most veteran members of the 41st had earned enough points in the army's rotation system to qualify for transfer home and out of the military. In fact, the 41st had been overseas and in combat for so long that family members of soldiers in its ranks had begun writing the war office and demanding the entire division be rotated home.[27]

Doyle Bruce who had been with Company G every day the unit had spent in combat had likely earned enough points for transfer before the unit's participation in the invasion of the Philippines. If not, the Purple Heart he earned for the wound he sustained during the fighting at Zamboanga qualified him. But filing reports took time and the problems of transportation and moving replacements to join the ranks of the 41st delayed rotation of veterans like Bruce until after the fighting on Bongao and Jolo was over.[28]

Bruce received word that he would be going home on April 24, 1945. His part in the war had almost come to an end. On his last night on Jolo, Bruce's company commander sent him on a night patrol putting his life at risk one last time. Bruce eventually forgave him, but he never forgot about it.[29]

CHAPTER 12

Japan and the End of the War

July 4, 1945–December 31, 1945

Within a few days of receiving word that he was being rotated home Sergeant Doyle Bruce boarded a ship headed for the United States. Just a few days before he got his orders to come home his mother received a telegram from the army informing her that her son had been wounded in combat. That telegram likely increased her anxiety about her son's health and safety. The delivery of another telegram a month later, this one from Bruce himself informing his family that he was on the way home, relieved her worry.[1]

From the Philippines Bruce traveled to San Francisco where he and the other soldiers were held over so the army could test their physical fitness before discharging them. According to Bruce that fitness test consisted of the men running around inside a gym in their underwear for a while. If a man could accomplish that, the army sent him on to a military base closer to his home. For Bruce this meant a train ride to San Antonio and Fort Sam Houston. The train he took carried a large number of men who had just returned from the war, and they spent most of the trip drinking. Bruce remembered that they were all so drunk when they arrived in San Antonio the army made them stay over an extra night so they could sober up before being formally discharged.[2]

Doyle Bruce received his honorable discharge on June 15, 1945.[3] He had served for three years and eight months and been overseas for three years and three months spending much of that time in combat. He earned the Combat Infantry Badge, the Distinguished Unit Badge, Asiatic Campaign Medal with three Bronze Stars, the Philippines

Liberation Medal with one Bronze Star, a Bronze Star Medal, and the Purple Heart with Oak Leaf Cluster.[4] He also carried the physical and mental scars that resulted from extensive combat in some of the worst conditions imaginable and chronic malaria.[5]

From San Antonio Bruce traveled to Houston where he stayed for a few days with his brother Victor Bruce who operated a crane at an ammunition plant on the Houston Ship Channel. His brother drove him to the family home in Lufkin, Texas where he was reunited with the rest of his family.

By the time the 2nd Battalion of the 163rd Infantry landed on the shores of Honshu, Japan, Doyle Bruce had reached his home in Texas I'm deleting/moving as essentially it's repeated in next line. He retrieved his blue 1940 Willys Coupe from his brother-in-law and settled into the civilian life many of his comrades in the army were still dreaming of having. A cousin who worked at Texas Foundry introduced Bruce to a young woman named Helen Slack and they went on a double date to a local dance hall where patrons had to bring their own food and booze. Helen made fried chicken and purple cabbage for their dinner. Doyle Bruce married Helen Slack on October 9, 1945.[6]

On July 4, 1945, the 162nd Regiment which had been attached to XX Corps as a part of the force eliminating the remaining Japanese resistance on Mindanao rejoined the rest of the division encamped around Zamboanga City.[7] As division veterans began to rotate home their replacements began arriving and preparing for the next combat mission—the invasion of Japan. Because of the significant number of new troops joining the ranks of the regiments, division command instituted a new and tough training program designed to prepare the men for their anticipated landing on the islands of Japan.

Those preparations ended when the United States dropped atomic bombs on the city of Hiroshima on August 6 and Nagasaki on August 9, annihilating both cities and killing tens of thousands of Japanese civilians. By August 15, the men of the 41st learned that because of the bombs the Japanese government had informed the United States that they were willing to accept the Allies' terms of surrender. The GIs celebrated what they hoped would be the end of the fighting. When the

Japanese officially surrendered the men were more subdued because by then, they had learned that some U.S. divisions would be used as a part of the occupation force that would be sent to Japan to oversee the surrender of thousands of Japanese soldiers and sailors. The soldiers of the 41st Division hoped to be sent home instead.[8]

On September 10, General Douglas MacArthur held a press conference in which he detailed which U.S. forces would make up the Army of Occupation. The 41st Division was among them. Allied command chose the 41st Division to occupy the area of Kure–Hiroshima on the western part of the island of Honshu.[9]

The 163rd's trip to Japan took place in two phases. The regiment boarded ships in the Philippines for Okinawa and, following a delay caused by a typhoon, sailed for Japan. The 2nd Battalion including Company G arrived first and established a shore base near the Japanese airstrip at Hiro where they began the work of unloading equipment and supplies. Once the other elements of the regiment arrived, the 2nd Battalion moved to their main base of operation east of Hiro.[10]

After routine but tense landings in early October, the various units of the 41st spread out across their assigned areas and began the work of disarming Japan. Their first tasks were logistical. Locations of camps and barracks had to be found and improved. Many of the Japanese barracks and warehouses selected for barracks were so unsanitary that army doctors would not allow the men to occupy them until they had been thoroughly cleaned, forcing some units to sleep in individual tents for weeks. Lieutenant Jack Anderson's Company G of the 186th landed near Kure on October 7, 1945, and moved with the rest of the 186th Regiment to the village of Kaidaichi just east of Hiroshima. Fleas had infested the warehouse Anderson's company was assigned as a barracks. The men could only get rid of them by saturating their sleeping bags with DDT.[11]

Once settled, the men conducted patrols in search of warehouses and other buildings that had been used by the Japanese military to store weapons and other military equipment. The Japanese government and military assisted the Americans in their destruction of the weapons, but only after the U.S. Army and individual soldiers took their pick.

Soldiers were allowed to take some of the materiel and send it home as trophies of war and each regiment and unit could take their pick as well. The army itself took some of the materiel for training purposes. The Americans returned those things they deemed to be safe to the Japanese or used it themselves. Most of the pistols, rifles, and other small arms and things like binoculars they destroyed.[12] For most of his time in Japan, Anderson's work kept him too busy destroying Japanese weapons and moving supplies for him to worry about how the occupation was going. He had two things on his mind—getting his job done and wondering when he would be eligible to return to the United States.[13]

The 41st also discovered and disposed of a large cache of chemical weapons that included thousands of toxic candles and large containers of toxic gas. The only way to quickly dispose of these materials was to dump them in the ocean. The Americans loaded the material on small Japanese ships crewed by former Japanese sailors but guarded by armed U.S. soldiers. The ships sailed out to sea a few miles and then the crew dumped everything overboard. This process was also used to dispose of other far less environmentally damaging material as well. Airplanes, airplane parts, artillery pieces, rifles, gunpowder, ammunition, and equipment that could be used to make those items were either destroyed or dumped.

The men of the 163rd's patrols and activities sometimes took them to Hiroshima, and they occasionally visited the area on leave. This meant that they were among the first Americans to witness the devastation caused by the atomic bomb. The way the bomb appeared to have stopped time left an impression on some of the men. Street cars blown off tracks with the skeletal remains of their passengers still inside and the strange shapes made by glass that had melted under the intense heat were sights that many men of the regiment remembered. Despite the devastation and the evidence of death and suffering, the men of the 163rd remained happy that the bomb had been dropped. The years spent fighting the Japanese in a ruthless and punishing war accounts for the harsh attitude of the American soldiers who believed the bomb had saved them from the death and injury that would have resulted from combat in Japan.[14]

Men of the 41st Division were stationed near Hiroshima during the American occupation of Japan and were among the first to tour the city after the dropping of the first atomic bomb, 1945. (National Archives)

Because of his unit's location near Hiroshima, Anderson had to make frequent trips through the ruins of the city to gather and deliver supplies. His first trip involved finding a route through the city that could be traversed by heavy trucks. He described the central part of the city as blown flat with only the twisted frames of a few buildings remaining. On a surviving tile wall, he saw the shadow left by a person who had been vaporized. He found that sheets of steel that looked solid turned to ash if touched. He only worried about radiation years later because the army had not warned the GIs or anyone else about the dangers.[15]

Demobilization of the Japanese military occupied part of the 41st Division's time in Japan as well. Nearly ninety percent of Japanese service men in the 41st's area of occupation demobilized before the division arrived in Japan. However, from October to December of 1945 the 41st processed the demobilization of almost 18,000 Japanese, most of whom returned to Japan from their overseas postings.

Japanese civilians were fearful of the American soldiers at first. The propaganda produced and distributed by the Japanese government

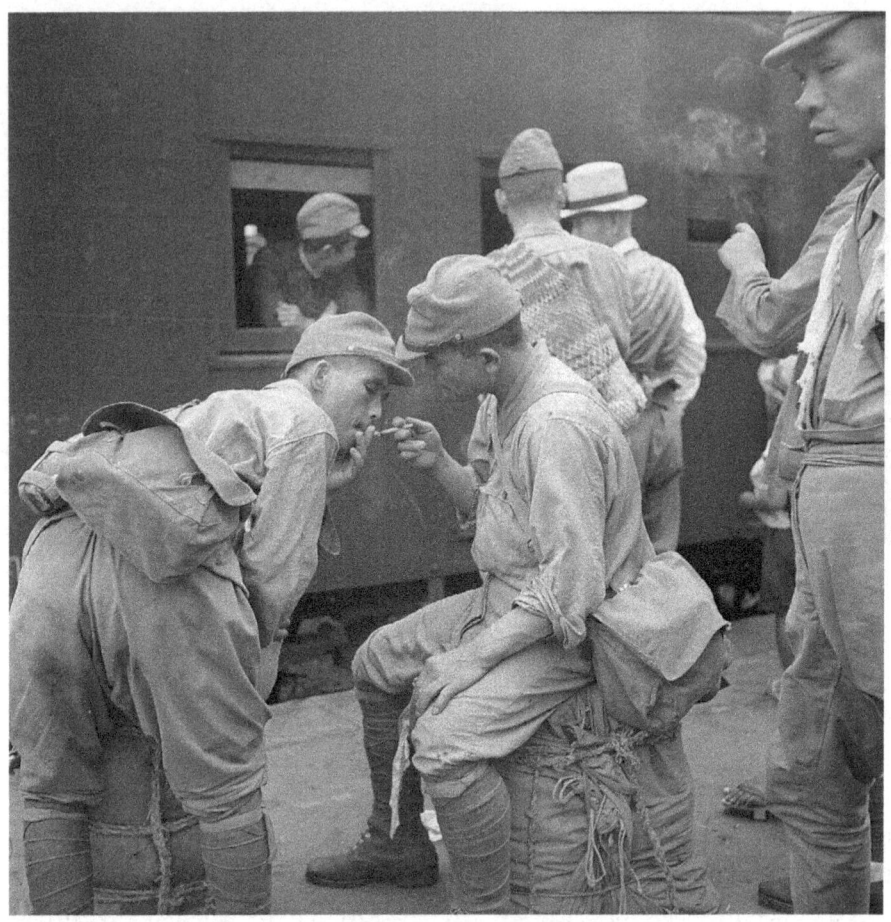

Demobilized Japanese soldiers made their way back to their home provinces to officially muster out of the army. (National Archives)

depicted Americans as monsters who would torture and kill them. Naturally, the people around Hiroshima and the survivors of the bomb were the most fearful. The men of the 41st received the full cooperation of the Japanese government and military officials, aiding the distribution of food to the near starving civilian population. There were complaints and disputes because of the slow distribution in the beginning, but eventually most of the supply problems were solved. By the time the 41st left Japan the Japanese civilians came to view the Americans in a neutral way—they realized the Americans were not there to kill them but to help them.[16]

At first, Anderson found the lack of any significant Japanese military presence unnerving, but he later learned that Japanese soldiers had returned to their home bases to await official orders telling them what to do. The participation of Japanese soldiers, sailors, and civilians in the gathering and disposal of weapons did not surprise Anderson. He believed their loyalty to the emperor meant that they did not question what they were told to do or believe they should harbor any ill will towards the Americans. If Emperor Hirohito told them to fight one day, they fought. If he told them to cooperate, they cooperated. In the days immediately following his landing in Japan, Anderson only caught glimpses of Japanese civilians and felt that their fear was based on what their government had led them to believe about Americans. They expected violence, death, and pain from Anderson and the other GIs. Instead, they got chewing gum, candy, and help. In time they came to depend on if not trust their American occupiers. Anderson felt real compassion for the Japanese civilians whom he believed had grown weary of the hardship and pain of the war and just longed for peace.[17]

Anderson received orders to transfer back to the U.S. in late October and boarded the USS *Falcon* on October 30 for the trip home. The ship arrived in San Francisco on November 11. It took a few days to complete the paperwork to get leave from the army to go home, but as soon as he was able, he returned home to Oregon where he married his sweetheart Betty Hallock on December 16. The malaria Anderson contracted in New Guinea returned a few days later and he spent a week in an army hospital recovering. Anderson's formal separation date from the army was December 24, 1945, but in January of 1946 he re-enlisted and became an instructor in the National Guard assigned to the 161st Infantry Regiment.[18]

By November, the American supply system in Japan had come fully online, and the food improved. The men settled into their new jobs, and many received word that they had earned enough points to transfer home. The cooks of the division prepared a full traditional American Thanksgiving dinner for the men and each man received a bottle of whiskey to make the holiday merrier. To fill the off time of the men stationed in Japan, the army provided recreational opportunities. The 41st fielded a division football and basketball team which won the

Occupation Forces championships. The army provided educational as well as recreational opportunities for the men. Courses ranging from electrical wiring to algebra, to psychology, to foreign languages gave the men a chance to learn skills and acquire knowledge that would either help the army or help them transition to civilian life.

No amount of fun, food, education, or booze could distract the men of the 41st from their obsession with finding out when the division would be deactivated. They received the news they were waiting for in late December. The 41st Division would be officially deactivated at midnight on December 31, 1945. With the division's deployment ended its men could begin making their way home.[19] For the men of Company G and all the other men of the 41st Division the war was finally over.

Epilogue

The war ended at different times for the four members of Company G whose stories make up the heart of this book. They returned to the United States with their bodies scarred by battle, their health diminished by disease and deprivation, and with memories of lost friends. With little to no fanfare they each settled into everyday life as quickly as they could.

Though Bruce Baird returned home ahead of many of the men from Company G, his time in the army did not come to an end until the war ended. He chose to join the Army Air Corps and transferred to a base in Wichita Falls, Texas. He married his longtime girlfriend while home in Ogden on emergency leave when his father died. After the funeral, the couple returned to Texas where they were allowed to live together off base. When the army realized that Baird had already earned enough combat points to rotate home, they informed him that he could not join the Air Corps and he transferred to a military hospital in Tampa, Florida, where he worked until the end of the war. After the war, Baird completed his college education and later he earned a PhD. He worked for a defense contractor that produced equipment for the Space Shuttle Program for twenty-five years. He and his wife had six children and twenty-nine grandchildren.[1]

During his service in the Pacific, Hargis Westerfield earned a Bronze Star and a Purple Heart, but he remained with Company G for the duration of the war and the occupation of Japan. Discharged on February 16, 1946, Westerfield left the army forever and married a young woman named Nancy. He went back to school and eventually earned a PhD from Indiana University. He taught English at the University of Nebraska at Kearny until he retired. As the official historian of the 41st Division, Westerfield organized reunions and published a quarterly division newsletter titled "The Jungleer" for many years. Some of their stories were collected by Westerfield and published in a volume titled *41st Infantry Division: Fighting Jungleers*. That book and the Hargis Westerfield Archive at the University of Montana form an incredible record of the 41st Division during World War II.[2]

When he returned home from service in World War II, Jack Anderson married his longtime sweetheart, Betty, but he re-enlisted almost immediately to train other young men for military service. With the outbreak of the Korean conflict, Anderson returned to active military service as an officer in the 38th Regiment of the 2nd Division. In seven months of fighting on the Korean Peninsula he was wounded, listed as missing in action, and became a prisoner of war. After returning home from his second war, Anderson settled in Lakewood, Washington, and raised three children with his wife Betty. He worked as a firefighter in that community for fifteen years and remained a devout Christian his entire life. He wrote a book about his life in the army during World War II and the Korean War that was published in 1997 titled *Warrior ...By Choice ...By Chance*.

After the war Doyle Bruce and his wife, Helen, lived for a short time in Houston before finally returning to their hometown of Lufkin, Texas. Bruce worked as a masonry contractor for 30 years before retiring. His reputation for toughness and his blue eyes earned him the nickname "Daddy Blue Eyes" from one of the men who worked for him. Many of the buildings he helped to build still stand in Lufkin and the surrounding communities and counties. Later on in life he sat for an interview with a relative in which he shared stories about his service in World War II and he kept a journal in which he included remembrances of the war. He and Helen had three children and five grandchildren. He remained a devoted husband, father, and Christian for the rest of his life.

Though some waited almost half a century, each of these men decided to share their stories of the war they fought in the mud, jungles, coral ridges, and mountain islands of the South Pacific. Some gave interviews and some wrote books, but each of their accounts relates the horror of war fought in the most difficult of circumstances and reflects their pride in their service in the 41st Division, 163rd Infantry's Company G.

Endnotes

Chapter 1

1   Anderson, Jack M. *Warrior ...By Choice ...By Chance: World War II, Korea* (Mukilteo, Washington, D.C.: Wine Press Publishing, 1997), 21–25.
2   McCartney, William F. *The Jungleers: A History of the 41st Infantry Division* (Nashville: The Battery Press, 1988), 1–21.
3   Kidston, Martin J. *From Poplar to Papua: Montana's 163rd Infantry Regiment in World War II* (Helena, Montana: Far Country Press, 2004), 4–5.
4   Anderson, *Warrior*, 25–32.
5   Anderson, *Warrior*, 41–45.
6   McCartney, *The Jungleers*, 6–13.
7   Bruce, Doyle Edward, Jr. *Doyle Edward Bruce 1916–1999: A Common Man of the Greatest Generation.* (Self-published, 2022), 27–28.
8   Baird, Bruce. "WWII and My Life With Military Duty In Australia, New Guinea, And USA." Bruce L. Baird Collection, Department of Special Collections, Utah State University Logan, Utah, 1–2.
9   McCartney, *The Jungleers*, 1–21.
10 Bruce, *A Common Man*, 27–28.
11 Baird, "WWII and My Life," 2–4.
12 Baird, "WWII and My Life," 4.
13 Kidston, *From Poplar to Papua*, 16–17.
14 McCartney, *The Jungleers*, 23–24.
15 Bruce, *A Common Man*, 28, 49.
16 Anderson, *Warrior*, 49–52.
17 Baird "WWII and My Life," 4.
18 Anderson, *Warrior*, 50–52.
19 Baird "WWII and My Life," 4.
20 Bruce, *A Common Man*, 28, 49.
21 Anderson. *Warrior*, 50–52.
22 McCartney, *The Jungleers*, 22–31; Anderson, *Warrior*, 52.
23 Bruce, *A Common Man*, 27–28, 51; Kidston, *From Poplar to Papua*, 21–21.
24 Kidston, *From Poplar to Papua*, 20–21.
25 Bruce, *A Common Man*, 50–51.

Chapter 2

1 Costello, John. *The Pacific War 1941–1945* (New York: Harper Collins Perennial, 2009), 219.
2 McCartney, *The Jungleers*, map on inside cover.
3 McCartney, *The Jungleers*, 25–26.
4 Baird, "WWII and My Life," 4.
5 McCartney, *The Jungleers*, 26.
6 Kidston, *From Poplar to Papua*, 22.
7 Anderson, *Warrior*, 54.
8 Baird, "WWII and My Life," 6.
9 Bruce, *A Common Man*, 56.
10 Baird, "WWII and My Life," 6.
11 McCartney, *The Jungleers*, 26–27.
12 Kidston, *From Poplar to Papua*, 22.
13 Kidston, *From Poplar to Papua*, 21–23.
14 Baird, "WWII and My Life," 5.
15 Kidston, *From Poplar to Papua*, 21–23.
16 Anderson, *Warrior*, 56.
17 Kidston, *From Poplar to Papua*, 24–26.
18 Anderson, *Warrior*, 54–55.
19 Anderson. *Warrior*, 52–62.
20 Baird, "WWII and My Life," 5.
21 Anderson, *Warrior*, 52–54.
22 McCartney, *The Jungleers*, 22–27.
23 Costello, *The Pacific War 1941–1945*, 318.
24 Bruce, *A Common Man*, 29.
25 Baird, "WWII and My Life," 6.
26 Anderson, *Warrior*, 53.
27 Baird, "WWII and My Life," 7.
28 Anderson, *Warrior*, 57.
29 Baird, "WWII and My Life," 7.
30 Kidston, *From Poplar to Papua*, 27–28.
31 McCartney, *The Jungleers*, 22–20.
32 Anderson, *Warrior*, 52–62.
33 Baird, "WWII and My Life," 7.
34 Anderson, *Warrior*, 52–62.
35 McCartney, *The Jungleers*, 27–28.
36 Anderson, *Warrior*, 52–62.
37 Baird, "WWII and My Life," 8.
38 Anderson, *Warrior*, 59.
39 Anderson, *Warrior*, 59–60.

40 Anderson, *Warrior*, 62.
41 Bruce, *A Common Man*, 29, 50–51; Anderson, *Warrior*, 64–65.
42 Anderson, *Warrior*, 60.
43 Costello, *The Pacific War 1941–1945*, 317–18.
44 Anderson, *Warrior*, 52–62.

Chapter 3

1   Costello, *The Pacific War 1941–1945*, 218–20.
2   Costello, *The Pacific War 1941–1945*, 249–63.
3   Costello, *The Pacific War 1941–1945*, 316–18.
4   Costello, *The Pacific War 1941–1945*, 374–81.
5   Anderson, *Warrior*, 68–69.
6   Bruce, *A Common Man*, 59.
7   Anderson, *Warrior*, 69–70.
8   Baird, "WWII and My Life," 8.
9   Anderson, *Warrior*, 69–70.
10 Anderson, *Warrior*, 70.
11 Bruce, *A Common Man*, 42.
12 Bruce, *A Common Man*, 42.
13 Bruce, *A Common Man*, 42.
14 Baird, "WWII and My Life," 9.
15 Anderson, *Warrior*, 70.
16 McCartney, *The Jungleers*, 33.
17 McCartney, *The Jungleers*, 32–37.
18 McCartney, *The Jungleers*, 32.
19 McCartney, *The Jungleers*, 36–37.
20 Baird, "WWII and My Life," 10.
21 McCartney, *The Jungleers*, 36–37.
22 Westerfield, Hargis, PhD. "163 Infantry: Counter-Sniping from Musket Perimeter," in *41st Infantry Division: Fighting Jungleers II*, Dr. Hargis Westerfield (Paducah, Kentucky: Turner Publishing, 1992), 17–18.
23 Anderson, *Warrior*, 77–78.
24 Baird, "WWII and My Life," 10–11.
25 Bruce, *A Common Man*, 69.
26 Anderson, *Warrior*, 71–73.
27 Anderson, Warrior, 71–74.
28 Westerfield, "The Killerton Road Block," 35–36.
29 Bruce, *A Common Man*, 56.
30 Westerfield, "The Killerton Road Block," 35.
31 Bruce, "WWII and My Life," 56.
32 Westerfield, "The Killerton Road Block," 35–36.

33 Bruce, *A Common Man*, 56.

34 Bruce, *A Common Man*, 56; Westerfield, "The Killerton Road Block," 36.

35 Westerfield, "The Killerton Road Block," 35–36.

36 McCartney, *The Jungleers*, 38.

37 McCartney, *The Jungleers*, 38.

38 Westerfield, Hargis PhD. "Infighting at Sanananda," in *41st Infantry Division: Fighting Jungleers II*, Dr. Hargis Westerfield (Paducah, Kentucky: Turner Publishing, 1992), 36–37.

39 McCartney, *The Jungleers*, 39.

40 Bruce, *A Common Man*, 57.

41 Anderson, *Warrior*, 87–89.

42 Westerfield, "Infighting at Sanananda," 37.

43 Baird, "WWII and My Life," 13.

44 Westerfield, "Infighting at Sanananda," 37.

45 Bruce, *A Common Man*, 58.

46 Baird, "WWII and My Life," 11–12.

47 Westerfield, "Infighting at Sanananda," 37.

48 Kidston, *From Poplar to Papua*, 69–72.

49 Westerfield, "Infighting at Sanananda," 37–38.

50 Baird, "WWII and My Life," 12.

51 Baird, "WWII and My Life," 9–13.

52 Bruce, *A Common Man*, 59.

53 Westerfield, "Infighting at Sanananda," 36–38.

54 Baird, "WWII and My Life," 14.

55 Baird, "WWII and My Life,"13–14.

56 McCartney, *The Jungleers*, 37–41.

57 Anderson, *Warrior*, 80.

58 Anderson, *Warrior*, 95.

59 McCartney, *The Jungleers*, 39.

60 Kidston, *From Poplar to Papua*, 56–57.

61 Bruce, *A Common Man*, 68.

62 Bruce, *A Common Man*, 30, 57–58, 80.

63 Bruce, *A Common Man*, 58.

64 Anderson, *Warrior*, 99–100.

Chapter 4

1 McCartney, *The Jungleers*, 41–42.

2 Westerfield, Hargis, PhD. "G Company 163 Infantry: The Kumusi Patrol," *41st Infantry Division: Fighting Jungleers II*, Dr. Hargis Westerfield (Paducah, Kentucky: Turner Publishing, 1992), 324–25.

3 Bruce, *A Common Man*, 89.

4   Anderson, *Warrior*, 107.
5   Bruce, *A Common Man*, 63.
6   Westerfield, "The Kumusi Patrol," 324–25.
7   Bruce, Helen. 2006. Interview with Brian Bruce.
8   Westerfield, "The Kumusi Patrol," 324–25.
9   Anderson, *Warrior*, 92–96.
10 Westerfield, "The Kumusi Patrol," 324–25.
11 Bruce, *A Common Man*, 56.
12 Westerfield, "The Kumusi Patrol," 324–25.
13 Anderson, *Warrior*, 106.
14 Baird, "WWII and My Life," 15–16.
15 Westerfield, "The Kumusi Patrol," 324–25.
16 Anderson, *Warrior*, 107.
17 Bruce, *A Common Man*, 58–61.
18 Westerfield, "The Kumusi Patrol," 324–25.
19 Anderson, *Warrior*, 107.
20 Westerfield, "The Kumusi Patrol," 324–25.
21 Bruce, *A Common Man*, 31.
22 Anderson, *Warrior*, 108.
23 Westerfield, "The Kumusi Patrol," 324–25.
24 Anderson, *Warrior*, 110.

Chapter 5

1   Anderson, *Warrior*, 109.
2   McCartney, *The Jungleers*, 51.
3   McCartney, *The Jungleers*, 44–48.
4   McCartney, *The Jungleers*, 51–69.
5   Kidston, *From Poplar to Papua*, 72–73.
6   McCartney, *The Jungleers*, 44–48.
7   Kidston, *From Poplar to Papua*, 82.
8   McCartney, *The Jungleers*, 44–48.
9   Kidston, *From Poplar to Papua*, 73–76.
10 McCartney, *The Jungleers*, 44–48.
11 Kidston, *From Poplar to Papua*, 79–84.
12 Anderson, *Warrior*, 109.
13 Anderson, *Warrior*, 112–17.

Chapter 6

1   McCartney, *The Jungleers*, 72.
2   Anderson, *Warrior*, 123.

3   Anderson, *Warrior*, 128.
4   Baird, "WWII and My Life," 17–19.
5   Anderson, *Warrior*, 124.
6   Baird, "WWII and My Life," 19.
7   Anderson, *Warrior*, 133–34.
8   Anderson, *Warrior*, 124–25.
9   McCartney, *The Jungleers*, 72.
10   Baird, "WWII and My Life," 19; United States Army. Service Record of Doyle Edward Bruce.
11   Anderson, *Warrior*, 123–25.
12   Baird, "WWII and My Life," 20–21.
13   Baird, "WWII and My Life," 19.
14   Anderson, *Warrior*, 128.
15   Anderson, *Warrior*, 130.
16   Anderson, *Warrior*, 130–32.
17   McCartney, *The Jungleers*, 70–72.
18   Anderson, *Warrior*, 135–37.
19   Bruce, *A Common Man*, 32.
20   Elizabeth Connellan, Gladstone, Australia, to Evie Bruce, Lufkin, TX, June 10, 1945. Correspondence. Photocopy. Collection of the Author, Friendswood, TX.

Chapter 7

1   Westerfield, Hargis, PhD. *41st Infantry Division: Fighting Jungleers II*, Dr. Hargis Westerfield (Paducah, Kentucky: Turner Publishing, 1992), 539.
2   McCartney, *The Jungleers*, 72–75.
3   Anderson, *Warrior*, 139.
4   Baird, "WWII and My Life," 21.
5   McCartney, *The Jungleers*, 72–75.
6   McCartney, *The Jungleers*, 77–87.
7   McCartney, *The Jungleers*, 89–91.
8   Bruce, *A Common Man*, 72.
9   Baird, "WWII and My Life," 21.
10   Anderson, *Warrior*, 150
11   Westerfield, Hargis, PhD. "G Co., 163 Infantry: The Marches of Aitape," *41st Infantry Division: Fighting Jungleers II*, Dr. Hargis Westerfield (Paducah, Kentucky: Turner Publishing, 1992), 96–97.
12   McCartney, *The Jungleers*, 89–91.
13   Baird, "WWII and My Life," 21–22.
14   Westerfield, "The Marches of Aitape," 96–97.
15   Baird, "WWII and My Life," 22.
16   Westerfield, "The Marches of Aitape," 96–97.

17 McCartney, *The Jungleers*, 89–91.
18 Westerfield, "The Marches of Aitape," 96–97.
19 McCartney, *The Jungleers*, 89–91.
20 Westerfield, "The Marches of Aitape," 96–97.
21 Westerfield, "The Marches of Aitape," 96–97.
22 Bruce, *A Common Man*, 73.
23 Anderson, *Warrior*, 151–52.
24 Baird, "WWII and My Life," 23.
25 Kidston, *From Poplar to Papua*, 97–99.
26 McCartney, *The Jungleers*, 89–91.
27 Westerfield, Hargis, PhD. "G Co., 163 Infantry: Patrol to Marok Village," *41st Infantry Division: Fighting Jungleers II*, Dr. Hargis Westerfield (Paducah, Kentucky: Turner Publishing, 1992), 98–99.
28 Anderson, *Warrior*, 147–48, 153.
29 Anderson, *Warrior*, 154.
30 Westerfield, "Patrol to Maroke Village," 98–99.
31 Kidston, *From Poplar to Papua*, 95–96.

Chapter 8

1   McCartney, *The Jungleers*, 93.
2   McCartney, *The Jungleers*, 93–94.
3   Westerfield, Hargis, PhD and Lt. Jack Arnold, "M Co., G Co., 163 Infantry: Tementoe Creek and Tor River," *41st Infantry Division: Fighting Jungleers II*, Dr. Hargis Westerfield (Paducah, Kentucky: Turner Publishing, 1992), 121–22.
4   Baird, Bruce L. Interviewed by Claudia Ross. USU Veterans History Project in association with the Library of Congress.
5   Westerfield and Arnold, "Tementoe Creek and Tor River," 121–22.
6   McCartney, *The Jungleers*, 93–94.
7   Kidston, *From Poplar to Papua*, 104–6.
8   McCartney, *The Jungleers*, 94–95.
9   Kidston, *From Poplar to Papua*, 108.
10 McCartney, *The Jungleers*, 95–97.
11 Kidston, *From Poplar to Papua*, 114.
12 McCartney, *The Jungleers*, 98–99.
13 Kidston, *From Poplar to Papua*, 113.
14 McCartney, *The Jungleers*, 99.
15 McCartney, *The Jungleers*, 99–101.
16 Baird, "WWII and My Life," 25.
17 Westerfield, Hargis, PhD. "163 Infantry Regiment: War of Nerves at Toem," *41st Infantry Division: Fighting Jungleers II*, Dr. Hargis Westerfield (Paducah, Kentucky: Turner Publishing, 1992), 123–24.

18 Baird, "WWII and My Life," 24.
19 Anderson, *Warrior*, 163–66.
20 Westerfield, "War of Nerves at Toem," 125.

Chapter 9

1   Anderson, *Warrior*, 175.
2   Bernstein, Marc D. *Hurricane at Biak: McArthur Against the Japanese May–August 1944.* (Marc D. Bernstein: 2000), 37–38.
3   Bernstein, *Hurricane at Biak*, 17–35.
4   Bernstein, *Hurricane at Biak*, 36–45.
5   McCartney, *The Jungleers*, 102–7.
6   Bernstein, *Hurricane at Biak*, 42.
7   McCartney, *The Jungleers*, 107.
8   McCartney, *The Jungleers*, 109.
9   McCartney, *The Jungleers*, 109–10.
10 McCartney, *The Jungleers*, 110–11.
11 McCartney, *The Jungleers*, 112–14.
12 McCartney, *The Jungleers*, 114–15.
13 McCartney, *The Jungleers*, 115–17.
14 McCartney, *The Jungleers*, 123–27.
15 McCartney, *The Jungleers*, 127.
16 Kidston, *Poplar to Papua*, 121–23.
17 Westerfield, Hargis, PhD. "Irving's Siege of Ibdi Pocket," *41st Infantry Division: Fighting Jungleers II*, Dr. Hargis Westerfield (Paducah, Kentucky: Turner Publishing, 1992), 187.
18 McCartney, *The Jungleers*, 110–21.
19 Anderson, *Warrior*, 177–79.
20 Westerfield, Hargis, PhD. "Ibdi Pocket and G Company" *41st Infantry Division: Fighting Jungleers II*, Dr. Hargis Westerfield (Paducah, Kentucky: Turner Publishing, 1992), 188–90.
21 Westerfield, "Ibdi Pocket," 188.
22 Anderson, *Warrior*, 179–83.
23 Bruce, *A Common Man*, 33–34, 75.
24 Kidston, *From Poplar to Papua*, 123–25.
25 Westerfield, Hargis, PhD. "G Company, 163 Infantry Deadly Patrols of 19 June 1944," 41st Infantry Division, Jungleer.com. From http://jungleer.com/new-guinea-campaign/biak?id=356. Accessed April 22, 2024.
26 Bruce, *A Common Man*, 34.
27 Westerfield, "Deadly Patrols of 19 June 1944."
28 Bruce, *A Common Man*, 33.
29 Westerfield, "Ibdi Pocket," 188–90.

30 McCartney, *The Jungleers*, 127, 130.

31 Westerfield, "Ibdi Pocket," 188–90.

32 Bruce, *A Common Man*, 33, 74.

33 Baird, "WWII and My Life," 26–27.

34 Westerfield, Hargis, PhD. "G Company 163 Infantry Assaults Ibdi Pocket," 41st Infantry Division, Jungleer.com. From http://jungleer.com/new-guinea-campaign/biak?id=357. Accessed April 22, 2024.

35 Westerfield, "Ibdi Pocket," 188–90.

36 McCartney, *The Jungleers*, 127–30.

37 Westerfield, "Ibdi Pocket," 188–90.

38 Westerfield, Hargis, PhD. "G Co. 163 Infantry: Mopping up on Biak," *41st Infantry Division: Fighting Jungleers II*. Dr. Hargis Westerfield (Paducah, Kentucky: Turner Publishing, 1992), 190–91.

39 Anderson, *Warrior*, 186.

40 Baird, "WWII and My Life," 22.

41 Westerfield, "Mopping up on Biak," 190–91.

42 Baird, "WWII and My Life," 27–28.

43 Anderson, *Warrior*, 191, 194–95.

Chapter 10

1 McCartney, *The Jungleers*, 133.

2 Anderson, *Warrior*, 227–28.

3 Anderson, *Warrior*, 210–17.

4 Anderson, *Warrior*, 228–30.

5 McCartney, *The Jungleers*, 133.

6 Anderson, *Warrior*, 235–36.

7 McCartney, *The Jungleers*, 136–39.

8 Anderson, *Warrior*, 232–36.

9 Anderson, *Warrior*, 236–38.

10 McCartney, *The Jungleers*, 133–42.

11 McCartney, *The Jungleers*, 143.

12 Westerfield, Hargis, "G Co. 163 Inf (2/Pn): Death Valley at Zamboanga," *41st Infantry Division: Fighting Jungleers II*, Dr. Hargis Westerfield (Paducah, Kentucky: Turner Publishing, 1992), 284.

13 Westerfield, Hargis, PhD. "Zamboanga: G Co., 163 Inf's Last Battle," *41st Infantry Division: Fighting Jungleers II*, Dr. Hargis Westerfield (Paducah, Kentucky: Turner Publishing, 1992), 217.

14 McCartney, *The Jungleers*, 143.

15 Kidston, *From Poplar to Papua*, 137–38.

16 Westerield, "Zamboanga," 217.

17 Bruce, *A Common Man*, 77–78.

18 McCartney, *The Jungleers*, 143–49.

19 Westerfield, "Death Valley," 284–86.

20 McCartney, *The Jungleers*, 143–47.

21 Westerfield, "Death Valley," 284–86.

22 McCartney, *The Jungleers*, 143–49.

23 Westerfield, Hargis, PhD and Clifton James Sr., "Headquarters Co., 1/Bn 163 Inf: Blow-up Hill and Pasonanca," *41st Infantry Division: Fighting Jungleers II*, Dr. Hargis Westerfield (Paducah, Kentucky: Turner Publishing, 1992), 214–15.

24 Kidston, *From Poplar to Papua*, 139–40.

25 Kidston, *From Poplar to Papua*, 139–40.

26 Westerfield, "Death Valley," 284–86.

27 Westerfield, "Zamboanga," 217.

28 Westerfield, "Death Valley," 285.

29 Westerfield, "Zamboanga," 217–18.

30 Westerfield, "Death Valley," 285.

31 Bruce, *A Common Man*, 79–80.

32 Kidston, *From Poplar to Papua*, 139–40.

33 Westerfield and James, "Blow-up Hill," 215–16.

34 Westerfield, "Zamboanga," 217–18.

35 McCartney, *The Jungleers*, 149.

36 McCartney, *The Jungleers*, 149.

37 McCartney, *The Jungleers*, 147–48.

38 Westerfield, "Death Valley," 285–86.

39 Westerfield, "Zamboanga," 217–18.

40 McCartney, *The Jungleers*, 148–49.

41 Westerfield, "Zamboanga," 217–18.

42 Westerfield, "Death Valley," 284–86.

43 Westerfield, "Zamboanga," 217–18.

44 Westerfield, "Death Valley," 284–86.

45 Bruce, *A Common Man*, 79–80.

46 Dulian, Kermit with Westerfield, Hargis, PhD. "G Co 163 Inf(2/Pln): Combat in the Zamboanga Ridges." *41st Infantry Division: Fighting Jungleers II*, Dr. Hargis Westerfield (Paducah, Kentucky: Turner Publishing, 1992), 466–68.

47 Dulian, "Combat," 466–68.

48 Westerfield, "Death Valley," 284–86.

49 Dulian, "Combat," 466–68.

50 Bruce, *A Common Man*, 78–79.

51 Westerfield, "Death Valley," 286.

52 Westerfield, "Zamboanga," 217–18.

53 Bruce, *A Common Man*, 79–80.

54 McCartney, *The Jungleers*, 148–49.

55 Dulian, "Combat," 466–68.

56 Bruce, *A Common Man*, 77–84.

57 Dulian, "Combat," 467.

58 Dulian, "Combat," 466–68.

59 Westerfield, "Zamboanga," 217–18.

60 Westerfield, "Zamboanga," 217–18.

61 Dulian, "Combat," 468.

62 Dulian, "Combat," 466–68.

63 McCartney, *The Jungleers*, 143–49.

64 Westerfield, "Blow-up Hill and Pasonanca," 216.

65 Maya, Rinnosuke, 2nd Lieutenant, 9th Air Brigade, Imperial Japanese army, Diary March 8, 1945–June 5, 1945. Translated by Headquarters Company, 41st Infantry Division, July 3, 1945. Hargis Westerfield Research Collection: 41st Infantry Division, Montana Historical Society, Helena Montana.

Chapter 11

1 Bruce, *A Common Man*, 35, 84–85.

2 McCartney, *The Jungleers*, 150–55.

3 McCartney, *The Jungleers*, 159–66.

4 McCartney, *The Jungleers*, 153.

5 Westerfield, Hargis, PhD with Kermit Dulian, "G Co's Bongao Action (Philippines)," *41st Infantry Division: Fighting Jungleers II*, Dr. Hargis Westerfield (Paducah, Kentucky: Turner Publishing, 1992), 450–52.

6 Westerfield, "Bongao Action," 450–52.

7 Westerfield, Hargis, PhD and Captain Robert Allen, "146 FA and 2/BN 163 Inf: Bongao and Sanga Sanga Islands," *41st Infantry Division: Fighting Jungleers II*, Dr. Hargis Westerfield (Paducah, Kentucky: Turner Publishing, 1992), 353.

8 Westerfield, "Bongao and Sanga Sanga," 353.

9 McCartney, *The Jungleers*, 152–53.

10 Westerfield, "Bongao Action," 450–51.

11 Westerfield, "Bongao and Sanga Sanga," 353.

12 Westerfield, "Bongao Action," 451–52.

13 Westerfield, "Bongao and Sanga Sanga," 353–54.

14 Westerfield, "Bongao and Sanga Sanga," 353–55; Kidston, *From Poplar to Papua*, 147–49.

15 Westerfield, "Bongao Action," 450–52.

16 Westerfield, Hargis, PhD. "163 Infantry Regiment: First Round at Jolo," *41st Infantry Division: Fighting Jungleers II*, Dr. Hargis Westerfield (Paducah, Kentucky: Turner Publishing, 1992), 226.

17 Westerfield, "Bongao Action," 450–52.

18 McCartney, *The Jungleers*, 152.

19 Kidston, *From Poplar to Papua*, 146–47.

20 McCartney, *The Jungleers*, 152–53.

21 Kidston, *From Poplar to Papua*, 147–49.

22 Westerfield, Hargis, PhD. "G Co 163 Inf-Classic Patrol on Jolo," *41st Infantry Division: Fighting Jungleers II*, Dr. Hargis Westerfield (Paducah, Kentucky: Turner Publishing, 1992), 233.

23 Westerfield, "Classic Patrol on Jolo," 233–34.

24 McCartney, *The Jungleers*, 153.

25 Bruce, *A Common Man*, 35.

26 Westerfield, Hargis, PhD. "163 Infantry Regiment: First Round at Jolo," *41st Infantry Division: Fighting Jungleers II*, Dr. Hargis Westerfield (Paducah, Kentucky: Turner Publishing, 1992), 226.

27 McCartney, *The Jungleers*, 156.

28 Bruce, *A Common Man*, 89.

29 Bruce, *A Common Man*, 35.

Chapter 12

1 Bruce, Doyle Edward Telegram to Betsy Rose Bruce, June 8, 1945.

2 Bruce, *A Common Man*, 67, 86–88, 95–100.

3 United States Army, Honorable Discharge of Doyle E. Bruce, June 15, 1945. Photocopy collection of Author.

4 United States Army, Honorable Discharge of Doyle E. Bruce. June 15, 1945.

5 Veterans Administration, "Award of Disability Compensation of Pension: Doyle E. Bruce."

6 Bruce, *A Common Man*, 67, 95–100.

7 McCartney, *The Jungleers*, 166.

8 McCartney, *The Jungleers*, 156–57.

9 McCartney, *The Jungleers*, 167.

10 McCartney, *The Jungleers*, 169.

11 Anderson, *Warrior*, 264–65.

12 McCartney, *The Jungleers*, 167–78.

13 Anderson, *Warrior*, 266.

14 Kidston, *From Poplar to Papua*, 155–57.

15 Anderson, *Warrior*, 266–68.

16 McCartney, *The Jungleers*, 174–75.

17 Anderson, *Warrior*, 265–66.

18 Anderson, *Warrior*, 269–71, 276.

19 McCartney, *The Jungleers*, 175–78.

Epilogue

1 Baird, "WWII and My Life," 28–34.

2 Westerfield, Hargis, PhD. *41st Infantry Division: Fighting Jungleers II* (Paducah, Kentucky: Turner Publishing, 1992), 539.

Bibliography

Anderson, Jack M. *Warrior …By Choice …By Chance: World War II, Korea.* Mukilteo, Washington, D.C.: WinePress Pub., 1997.

Baird, Bruce. "WWII and My Life With Military Duty In Australia, New Guinea, And USA." Bruce L. Baird Collection, Department of Special Collections, Utah State University Logan, Utah.

Bernstein, Marc D. "Hurricane at Biak: McArthur Against the Japanese May–August 1944" (master's thesis, San Jose State University, 1999).

Bruce, Doyle Edward, Jr. *Doyle Edward Bruce 1916–1999: A Common Man of the Greatest Generation.* Self-published, 2022.

Costello, John. *The Pacific War 1941–1945.* New York: Harper Collins Perennial, 2009.

Kidston, Martin J. *From Poplar to Papua: Montana's 163rd Infantry Regiment in World War II.* Helena, Montana: Far Country Press, 2004.

Maya, Rinnosuke, 2nd Lieutenant, 9th Air Brigade, Imperial Japanese Army. "Diary March 8, 1945–June 5, 1945. Translated by Headquarters Company, 41st Infantry Division, July 3, 1945." Hargis Westerfield Research Collection: 41st Infantry Division, Montana Historical Society, Helena, Montana.

McCartney, William F. *The Jungleers: A History of the 41st Infantry Division.* Nashville: The Battery Press, 1988.

Westerfield, Hargis, ed. *41st Infantry Division: Fighting Jungleers II.* Paducah, Kentucky: Turner Publishing, 1992.

Index

Note: Italicized page numbers denote images.